A Brief History

Putney &
Roehampton

By Scott MacRobert
and The Putney Society

Designed and printed by aquatint|bsc

C O N T E N T S

INTRODUCTION

1.	Beginnings	1
2.	The Middle Ages	10
3.	Putney Under the Tudors	13
4.	Parish and Parks	17
5.	The Putney Debates 1647	22
6.	To Build a Bridge?	28
7.	Highways, Travellers and Highwaymen	33
8.	Roehampton 15th to 21st Century	37
9.	Growth Begins	60
10.	Saving the Commons	69
11.	Literature and Leisure	74
12.	Putney at War 1939-45	83
13.	Putney and the Seventies	90
14.	Bestride the Millennium	93
	REFERENCES AND NOTES ON THE TEXT	103

M A P S

Roman Putney   5
after Fuentes (1993.)

Putney 1636   25
Nicholas Lane

Putney 1787   35
By John Corris. Plan of Putney Parish

Parish of Putney 1859*   61
From a Report on the charities of Putney

Putney 1862*   65
From Stanford Library Map of London

Putney 1899   77
From Wandsworth and Putney Gas Co's Distribution Map

Second World War Map*   85

*Maps: Wandsworth Libraries Local History Collection

PHOTOS AND ILLUSTRATIONS

Small flint hand-axe from Dover House Road*   42

Mesolithic flint microliths from Sefton Street   42

(photo: Stan Warren)

Timber fish trap or fish weir on the Putney foreshore*   56

WHS Collections WM 977-05

The Agreement of the People   41

(Courtesy of Worcester College, Oxford)

The Old Putney Bridge in l880*   44

Last pictures of the old Putney Bridge and Aqueduct. 1884*   45

Putney Bridge Toll House 1879.*   48

Putney Embankment 1895*   49

Putney High Street 1880*   52

Putney High Street 1936*   53

Wandsworth Libraries Local History Collection

Pillbox, Putney Bridge Station*   43

Winchester House, Putney Embankment*   46

Manresa House, Roehampton*   47

Mount Clare, Roehampton*   50

Alton Estate, Roehampton*   51

Roehampton House, Queen Mary Hospital, Roehampton*   54

Blue plaques*   55
Lord Jenkins, Gavin Ewart, Norman Parkinson
Green plaque: Clement Attlee
Sundial: Zeeta House, Upper Richmond Road

photography by Trevor Sutters

Trevor Sutters, DipArch, RIBA, FRSA, ACArch is a practising architect who was commissioned by the Putney Society to take photographs for this edition of the Putney History. He has a keen interest in photography, composition and design. His work which spans buildings and interiors of both contemporary and traditional form can be viewed at www.sutterspartnership.co.uk.

INTRODUCTION

This short history was originally written as an examination thesis by a young South African student of architecture, Scott MacRobert. Scott, who died in 1975, was an active member of The Putney Society. The Putney Society is grateful to Mrs Joan MacRobert, Scott's mother, for kindly donating the copyright of the original work to the Society.

This book is intended as a short, popular account of the history of Putney and its civic development. The Society works closely with the Wandsworth Historical Society and is grateful for its assistance in this account as well as permission to quote from its research.

This new edition has been edited by Sue Rolfe, with new material by John Ewing, Dorian Gerhold, Pamela Greenwood, John Horrocks, Richard Morgan, and Hugh Thompson.

EDITOR'S NOTE

Chapters have been updated and contributed by a number of subject specialists and therefore reflect a variety of styles.

CHAPTER ONE
Beginings

Scott began his account with a description of his visit to an excavation by Wandsworth Historical Society at Sefton Street, probably in 1969, so starting his own journey of discovery of early Putney:

> In a short residential street near Putney Common is a building site screened from the road by a corrugated-iron hoarding. Behind it is a litter of builders' rubble and mounds of earth. A rectangular hole occupies part of the site and it was this hole or excavation which I visited on a recent wet Sunday afternoon.

> Here was a group of people (members of the Archaeological Group of the Wandsworth Historical Society) scraping carefully at the sand and examining every minute scrap of stone or pottery…

Archaeological excavations began in Putney in 1962, sparked off by the find of two Roman cremation burial urns and at least three other pots in the garden of 4 Bemish Road which are now in the Museum of London (WHS Newsletter 1962 No 2; Celoria 1965, 141 and plate 1). A number of digs followed, mostly in the area just west of the High Street, and within ten years had revealed a substantial area of Roman settlement and its road system, a small but interesting amount of prehistoric evidence, as well as that from medieval and later periods.[1] Many ancient objects have been recovered from the Thames since the 19th century, some from the foreshore and some by dredgermen. Wandsworth Historical Society and others continue to examine the foreshore, a zone rich in new information about early Putney. Environmental samples and studies too are giving us a better understanding of the Thames in the past.

Gradually a picture is emerging of Putney's distant past, drawn from all the different strands of evidence. Putney owes its importance to its geographical position by the Thames, at a point where it could be crossed relatively easily by ford, ferry or bridge without having large areas of marsh. Additionally, its riverside alluvial soils are good for agriculture and are easy to work. Fishing would have been important in some periods but, interestingly, current national evidence suggests not in the Neolithic (Schulting 2008, 104).

It is only since the Anglian stage of the Ice Age, about 500,000 years ago, when the glacier reaching as far south as Hampstead and Upminster diverted the Thames, then much larger, from its course out towards Clacton that it has flowed in its present valley (Sumbler 1996; Wymer 1991; 1999; Barron et al 2008). Then Putney would have been more like the Arctic and tundra of today. Subsequent alternating cold and warm periods led to the alternate cutting down of the riverbed and deposition of sands and gravels, so forming the stepped terraces of the local valley sides that we see today. Occasionally, flint hand-axes made by the earliest humans in the area have been found locally, for example from the Thames at Putney or on dry land in Keswick Road (Wymer 1968; 1999; Lewis 2000a). These generally date from 450,000-250,000 years ago. The most recent dry-land find, from an allotment in Dover House Road, is a small, typically Neanderthal style hand-axe (8. centrefold) dated to 128-75,000 years ago, again a period of extreme cold conditions (Bird, C, 1977; Greenwood 1986a, 6). It is similar to others found in the area (Wymer 1968; Sumbler *et al* 1996). Traces of the earliest modern humans, around from 40,000 years ago when Britain was still very cold, are very rare everywhere, including Putney (Lewis 2000b). Peat deposits dating to end of this period, about 8200-5600 cal BC at Barn Elms and 9000-6000 cal BC at Point Pleasant, give us some idea of the boggy conditions by the river and of the local pine woodland.[2]

After the end of the last cold phase of the Ice Age, about 12,000-10,000 years ago, the Thames slowly began to assume its present course. Sea-levels then were considerably lower than today and the river was formed of many channels until sometime during the Bronze Age when it began to take on its current line and shape. Around 5000-4000 BC the Thames was still a broad, shallow river flowing moderately fast, though much lower than today, perhaps 3m or more below present low tides (Sidell and Wilkinson 2004). By the end of the Bronze Age, about 800 BC, the Thames had become tidal in central

London. Here at Putney, evidence suggests that it still was freshwater and perhaps never higher than the lowest tides today, the present foreshore being dry land or an intermediate wet and dry zone (Sidell and Wilkinson 2004).

The Sefton Street site (Warren 1977) is the only extensive area of Stone Age evidence investigated so far. Here archaeologists uncovered scatters of flint implements and knapping waste. Some had been made by late Mesolithic hunter-gatherers (c 7000-4000 BC) (see page 42). However, the bulk of the flint, some hundreds of pieces, was that knapped by the first farmers of the earlier Neolithic (c 4200-2900 BC) who also left behind a few fragments of pottery. Early Mesolithic (c 8500-6000 BC) evidence is better known from the foreshore downstream of the Bridge, as are finds of Mesolithic flint adzes for wood-working, commonly known as 'Thames picks' (Wymer 1977; Greenwood 1986b; 1988; WHS Colls; MoL Colls). Late Mesolithic microlithic implements occur in small numbers on many Putney sites.

The decorated pieces of Neolithic pottery from Putney, and therefore all the more easily identifiable, belong to the middle Neolithic Mortlake/Fengate tradition with a revised dating to 3300-2800 cal BC (Greenwood 1987; Cotton with Johnson 2004, 133). An early Neolithic flint-knapper's hearth from Felsham Road and pottery and flints from Bemish Road, The Platt area and Kingsmere Close show Neolithic settlement and activity spread out along the riverside west of the High Street at about the 3-6m contour. Identifiable Neolithic evidence from the modern foreshore is sparse – some pottery, flint tools and the occasional polished or ground stone axe (also found on dry land, for example from Putney Common). This may reflect casual activity rather than settlement along the river banks. Late Neolithic (c 2900-2200 BC) evidence as a whole is also sparse. In the London area the general vegetation in the Neolithic period was oak and hazel on lower slopes and alder carr along the Thames (Sidell 2007, 71).

While we have very few traces of people of the early Bronze Age (c 2200-1700 BC) from present day Putney on dry land, apart from a few flint implements, a small number of stone axes and bronze axes and spearheads have come from the river zone. Tantalizingly, a place-name close to the Beverley Brook is marked on Nicholas Lane's 1636 map of Putney as 'Ringesmere Hills'[3]. Could this be the site of some early Bronze Age round barrows? The location is a typical one for such barrows as at Ham (Needham 1987).

After the sparse early Bronze Age finds, the middle (c 1700-1150 BC) and late Bronze Age (c 1150-800 BC) present a great contrast. Finds recovered from the foreshore or by dredging comprise a number of rapiers, axes, spearheads and swords, often found in clusters, especially between Putney Bridge and the Wandle (Rowlands 1976, 207)[4]. A few fragments of middle Bronze Age pottery (WHS Colls) and a broken spearhead (R. Wells Colls) found just downstream of the eastern Putney parish boundary may indicate a settlement. Similarly, late Bronze Age metalwork and pottery (WHS Colls; R.Wells Colls) around the boundary may point to a late Bronze Age one. Some dry land and foreshore finds by the mouth of the Beverley Brook suggest another late Bronze Age or earliest Iron Age site, perhaps 1000-800 BC (WHS Colls). At Felsham Road a few postholes and small pits produced pottery fragments and flint implements dating to around 800 BC. There are some indications that part of the current foreshore was dry land in this period – sea levels were lower and deliberately damaged or broken swords have been found on the foreshore. Swords buried on dry land, perhaps easier to recover, were rendered unusable before being deposited as shown in a study by Quilliec (2008).

Scott mentions Caesar's Camp on Wimbledon Common, acknowledging that it is "misleadingly known as Caesar's Camp" since it was an Iron Age fort. It dates to the beginnings of the Iron Age, around 800-750 BC and overlooks this part of the valley down to the Thames (Lowther 1945; Merriman 1990).

Discoveries from the early 1970s onwards have revealed much more about Iron Age Putney than was previously known from the antiquarian river finds. Increasing amounts of pottery probably dating to the earliest Iron Age (8th-6th centuries BC) are being found downstream of Putney Railway Bridge, suggesting a settlement or some activity at the very least along former banks of the Thames. A recent find of a fine, burnished and decorated bowl raises some interesting questions as elsewhere such pots are found in dumps or special deposits, for example on some east London sites (Greenwood 1997; Greenwood et

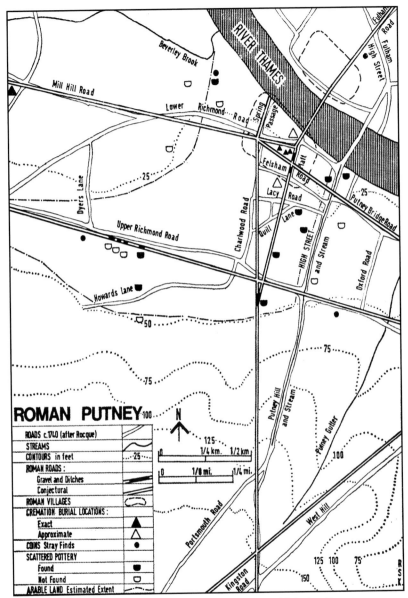

The map contains the following text labels:

RIVER THAMES

Beverley Brook

Fulham Road

High Street

Mill Hill Road

Lower Richmond Road

Spring Passage

Dyers Lane

25

Felsham Road

Platt

Charlwood Road

Lacy Road

Quill Lane

HIGH STREET

and Stream

Putney Bridge Road

25

Oxford Road

Upper Richmond Road

Howards Lane

50

75

75

Putney Hill and Stream

Pinney Gutter

100

ROMAN PUTNEY 100

N

125

1/4 km. 1/2 km.

1/8 mi. 1/4 mi.

ROADS c.1740 (after Rocque)	
STREAMS	
CONTOURS in feet	...25...
ROMAN ROADS :	
Gravel and Ditches	
Conjectural	
ROMAN VILLAGES	
CREMATION BURIAL LOCATIONS :	
Exact	▲
Approximate	△
COINS Stray Finds	●
SCATTERED POTTERY	
Found	▄
Not Found	▽
ARABLE LAND Estimated Extent	

Portsmouth Road

West Hill

Kingston Road

125 100 75

150

R S K

Roman Putney – Actual and Conjectural by Nicholas Fuentes
updated for this work

al 2006; Brudenell 2008). An early Iron Age settlement, dating to the 5-4th centuries BC,[5] was discovered in 1974 by the Beverley Brook at Barn Elms during construction of the river-defence wall. Nearby, a large pit and other evidence of the middle Iron Age (c 400-150 BC) were excavated on the site of the Gas Pipeline Terminal (BEV I). This site and nearby finds, particularly of potin coins,[6] indicate a major settlement around here in the late 2nd or early 1st century BC (Greenwood 1997). A fragment of a mature man's skull found in 2003 between the bridges on the Putney foreshore has now been radiocarbon dated to around 400 cal BC (Cotton and Green 2004, 135-6; Bob Wells pers.com). Unfortunately we cannot tell if he was a local man.

Apart from the concentration of Iron Age evidence around the Beverley Brook, a tantalizing glimpse of other potential areas is provided by fragments of a middle Iron Age bowl from Bemish Road and of late Iron Age cup and 1st-century AD strainer bowl, neither Roman in tradition, from an early ditch in the Roman settlement area in Felsham Road. River finds, including pottery, a dagger and a bead show that people were in the area throughout the Iron Age (WHS Collections; Cotton and Wood 1996). An early 1st-century AD Roman sword with an elaborate scabbard, the 'Fulham Sword', found in the Thames, and now in the British Museum (BM 1883,0407.1), could have been lost by a conquering legionary, but again it might have been acquired by a local Iron Age resident.

Roman Putney was excavated piecemeal as redevelopment took place from 1962-1986. In the current state of knowledge, the heart of the settlement lies to the west of the High Street from the Star and Garter area to Spring Passage with Roman material and activity being found as far west as Danemere Street (WHS Newsletter 1973 no105) (Roman Map). The settlement appears to have expanded during the Roman period. The first Roman road discovered in 1966 led towards the river under The Platt, now renamed Thames Place. A shorter road in the same position is shown on Nicholas Lane's 1636 map. Later excavations off Gwendolen Avenue, behind the old Putney Police Station, identified this Roman road's probable junction with another road apparently leading down to the river by Spring Passage, a suggested location for a ford. Four or five sections of an ancient metalled road on the line of the present Upper Richmond Road have now been found from the High Street westwards, all with few finds but of Roman style construction. After further excavations, mostly within the Roman settlement area, Nicholas Fuentes collated and assessed the different levels of evidence for the roads, such as Roman finds and burials, later place-names and documentary sources. He produced the reconstruction of the local Roman road system and river-crossings shown here while reminding us that many of the possible roads or their extensions remain conjectural (Roman Map)[7]. All the excavated roads had gravelled surfaces. The Platt Roman road had a very long life-span, producing some Roman pottery from its roadside ditches which could date into the early 400s. Coins from the settlement range in date from AD 79 to around 400, though the pottery indicates mid-1st century AD beginnings. A hoard of worn Roman coins found on the foreshore by Wandsworth Park (Ron Caddy pers.com), the bulk minted from AD 388-402 (Hammerson and Hall 1987), adds to the evidence for the late survival of the settlement here as these must have been in circulation for some time.

Excavations at Roman Putney have revealed small timber buildings and other structures, land division and fields, farming – cattle, pig, horse and sheep/goat bones, the use of wild resources such as red deer antler, and the bones of a red kite.[8] Several spindlewhorls are evidence of spinning and weaving cloth. Charcoal fragments from Bemish Road were identified as chestnut, oak, ash, hazel, hornbeam and elm wood. Large quantities of slag from Bemish Road and Felsham Road, as well as fragments of furnace wall and holes for the nozzles of bellows from Felsham Road, are debris left by the settlement's blacksmiths. Iron objects include a ladle, latch lifter and many nails. Roman Putney was a prosperous roadside settlement, probably in control of the river crossing, importing pottery from elsewhere in Britain, as well as goods from the Continent, such as amphorae (large jars for wine, oil and fish sauce), glossy samian pottery from Gaul and Germany and lava quernstones (rotary hand-mills for grinding flour) also from Germany. The inhabitants lost a number of coins, brooches, hairpins, bracelets and military-type fittings (WHS excavations; Fuentes and Greenwood 1993) and possibly even a shoe – part of one was found on the foreshore (BM 1984, 0603.1). The only definite votive or religious item recognised so far is a broken pipeclay figurine of Venus (Slade 1980). Large pits, often rich in finds, or sometimes dumps in ditches are typical of the 1st and 2nd centuries AD. In contrast, in the late Roman phase pottery and other finds tend to be found in ditches, small pits or spread about, disturbed by later ploughing, perhaps reflecting a change from large pits to dung heaps or tips for rubbish disposal.

1st or 2nd – century AD cremation burials in pots have been found alongside the Roman roads at The Platt and Coopers Arms Lane, now Lacy Road (WHS excavations and archive). The group from Bemish Road is later, 3rd-4th century AD in date (Celoria 1965; Lyne and Jeffries 1979, 72). An old report mentions a Roman urn from Point Common, once near the modern Duke's Head public house, just west of The Platt Roman road (Fuentes 1991, 16, 25 note 7). So far no inhumation burials of any kind have been discovered. The nearest known are four from Battersea, including one skeleton in a lead coffin (Fuentes 1989b), clearly someone of substance. There is an intriguing reference in an antiquarian report to twenty three barrows beside the present A3 near Tibbett's Corner. Apart from mentioning Roman vessels, it has a drawing of a pot of Roman appearance unearthed from one of the barrows (WHS Finds Index; Fuentes 1994, 12).

Along the foreshore from the Beverley Brook, the Beaver brook (Coles 2006, 154-5), to the river Wandle, where a beaver-bone was found in mid-Roman deposits (James Rackham unpublished notes), there is a scatter of Roman finds, increasing in quantity downstream of the railway bridge suggesting further settlement along the river towards Wandsworth. While there is some evidence of today's Putney foreshore still being dry land during the Roman period, recent samples from the area by the Wandle mouth indicate that this area was water-meadow around AD 220-440, gradually becoming marshy with peat forming in the period AD 430-660 (Perry and Skelton 1996; Cowie and Blackmore 2008, Table 73; Rackham and Scaife 1997; Sidell 2008).

It is not clear what became of the settlement at Putney in the early 5th century AD after the secular administration from Rome ended, though there were clearly people in the area and no particular excavated evidence of destruction here or in Surrey. A fish trap or weir, downstream of the Railway Bridge, opposite Deodar Road, gave radiocarbon dates from two of its timbers, one oak and the other elm, in the range AD 410-640 (Greenwood 2008; Cowie and Blackmore 2008, Table 73). Its timbers can be seen at very low tide (see page 56). This dating partly overlaps that of the late Roman coin hoard found nearby. As well as a few late coins, some of the Roman pottery from the Putney settlement potentially has a very late date range, the production of certain types continuing sometime after AD 400, perhaps into the 430s (Malcolm Lyne pers. com; Lyne and Jeffries 1979; Tyers website). Much more needs to be done to understand the period from AD 400-450 and before any other changes in the late 5th century. It is clear, however, from the archaeology of early Putney that areas of human activity and settlement shifted over time not always showing exact continuity on the same piece of land. In reality a very small area has been excavated and studied and almost every site has produced fresh evidence or a different combination of periods, such as would never have been expected before 1962.

CHAPTER TWO
The Middle Ages

The first written reference to Putney is in the Domesday Book of 1086, in the entry for Mortlake manor (later known as Wimbledon manor), which belonged to the Archbishop of Canterbury. The reference is to "twenty shillings from the toll of the vill of Putelei". This was probably the income from a ferry and perhaps fees for other boats landing. Putney was mentioned only because this part of the manor's income came from Putney alone, and it is likely that many of the villeins and cottagers recorded for the manor as a whole were in fact farming at Putney. Unfortunately the Domesday Book was not a census, and does not provide a clear indication of Putney's population.

The absence of written references to Putney before 1086 does not mean that it did not exist. There was little need to write about a settlement which was neither a manor nor a parish. Even archaeological evidence is notoriously elusive for the Anglo-Saxon period. In fact the exciting recent discovery of a fish trap on the Thames foreshore near Wandsworth Park suggests that occupation continued after the Roman period. The fish trap was a double row of posts (one with at least 45 posts). Other finds include a Saxon axe in Felsham Road. Also, the detached part of Putney parish by the river in Barnes, consisting of highly-valued meadow land, cannot have come into existence later than 950, when Barnes was separated from Mortlake manor.

In the Domesday Book Putney is called *Putelei*. Unless this was merely an error by a Norman scribe, it meant *Putta's clearing*. *Putta* was a personal name of the time (there was a Bishop of Rochester called *Putta*;[1] and the name may survive in the surname Potter). Who was *Putta*? It has often been assumed that he was a Saxon chieftain or noble, but, apart from a desire to establish an honourable founder of Putney, there is no reason to suppose that he was anything of the sort. He may have been merely the ferry-owner. The name usually recorded, starting with the second reference to Putney in 1279, was

Puttenhuth,[2] meaning *Putta's landing-place.* It commemorated what was clearly Putney's most distinctive feature.

A document of 1291 discovered in the archives of Lincoln Cathedral provides the first reference to a church at Putney. Excavations in 1975-6 uncovered the foundations of the thirteenth century church. Remarkably, this church, with extensions and internal adaptations such as galleries, continued to serve the community right up to 1836, when the population was far larger. The surviving tower dates from about 1500. The church was not a parish church: it was a chapel of ease to the parish church in Wimbledon, though Putney was nevertheless often referred to as a parish, even in legal documents.

Many of the village's inhabitants must still have engaged in activities relating to the river. Fishing and ferrying continued to be a major part of the community's economy until much later. But others would have worked in the fields. Putney's field names provide some evidence of an early pattern of scattered farms and enclosed fields. But Putney eventually acquired open fields divided into narrow strips, probably in the tenth or eleventh centuries. When the layout of the fields is first recorded in the fifteenth century, there is not the pattern common in the Midlands of three fields of similar size. Instead there were six open fields of varying sizes. They are listed in a detailed *terrier* (a record of landowners and their lands) as follows:

BASTON FIELD
70.5 ACRES

North: The Thames

West: Properties on east side of High Street

South: Upper Richmond Road

East: Boundary with Wandsworth

COALECROFT FIELD
94.25 ACRES

North: Upper Richmond Road

West: Putney Hill

South: Putney Heath Lane

East: Boundary with Wandsworth

SMALLTHORN & WADDON 42.75 ACRES	FOURTH FIELD 86.5 ACRES
North: Fifth Field	North: Fifth Field
West: Fourth Field	West: Putney Park
South: The Heath	South: The Heath
East: Putney Hill	East: Smallthorn & Waddon

FIFTH FIELD 88.25 ACRES	SIXTH FIELD 216.75 ACRES
North: Upper Richmond Road	North: The Thames
West: Putney Park	West: Putney Lower Common
South: Third and Fourth Fields	South: Upper Richmond Road
East: Smallthorn & Waddon	East: Properties on west side of High Street

Three of the fields had no name, but each field consisted of a number of shots and each of these did have its own name. This suggests that the shot was the land division which was generally spoken of. It was between the shots or groups of shots that rotation of crops would have been practised, though when animals grazed the land they could wander freely within a whole field.[3] The shots were divided into strips which were distributed among the manor's tenants, each one of whom held a number of scattered strips.

Another medieval feature was the manorial park known as Putney Park, first recorded in 1273-4. Its main purpose was to supply venison and other produce for the Archbishop's manor house at Mortlake. Its bounds were Upper Richmond Road in the north, the western boundary of the Dover House Estate in the west, Putney Heath in the south and the present Larpent Avenue in the east.

CHAPTER THREE

Putney under the Tudors

With the Tudors came an age of prosperity and peace; an age when a man building a house thought more of convenience than of defence. Travel became safer and, as the economy of the country took on a more dynamic character, travel became more necessary. And with the growth of travel so Putney grew too. Scattered references in contemporary documents point to the relationship between the growth of Putney and the opening up of the routes on which it depended for much of its prosperity. For example, there is recorded in the Privy Purse Expenses of 12 June 1531 a payment of 10s 8d to the King's watermen for "waiting with the barge to Putney with 16 men"[1]. And similarly in the Queen's Payments of August 1544 a payment of 8d is recorded for the hire of a boat from Westminster to Putney when she removed from Westminster to Hampton Court[2].

The significance of the ferry at Putney is not immediately obvious to us today since we are so accustomed to road transport, but road travel in Tudor times was often dangerous and unpleasant and people preferred to travel by water wherever possible.

It has already been noted in connection with prehistoric times how Putney's geographic situation made it an ideal point for a river crossing or landing. This fact was every bit as evident in Tudor and Stuart times as it had been in the days of the Romans.

Two routes developed from London or Westminster into south and south-west England: the one was along the north of the river (the modern Fulham Road) and so over the river by ferry to Putney; the other was by river to Putney. There was a third route if you were Royalty: you had a private road – literally; the King's Road, through Chelsea and Fulham was the King's private road. But even Royalty had to cross the river and pass through Putney.

There were two kinds of ferry: a short-haul ferry which operated between Fulham and Putney, and a long-distance ferry plying between Putney and London or Westminster.

Information about the ferry is often indirect. It is said, for example, that one night the Bishop of London was crossing from Putney to his palace at Fulham when he, his horses and his retinue were emptied into the river[3]. An enlightening reference to the ferry is to be found in the Journal of James Yonge, surgeon, of Plymouth (1647–1721):

> Sunday 23 May 1686. Sir Charles Carny and I rode from Guildford to London in my Lord Dartmouth's coach. We ferried over Putney passage, the coach and six horses together in the boat, and we in it, so that I rode over the Thames[4].

This shows that some of the short-haul ferries were capacious craft, probably flat-bottomed pontoons in fact. Rowing or paddling a craft of this size and shape would not have been easy and they may have been poled over the water like a punt. This may have limited crossings to middle and low tides since the tidal range at Putney is considerable.

The long-haul ferry was probably a more conventional sort of boat.

Other documents tell us more: thus during the forty-second year of the reign of Elizabeth it was decreed that if the watermen should neglect to pay to the ferry-owner a halfpenny for every stranger and a farthing for every inhabitant of Putney crossing the river, they would forfeit two shillings and six pence to the Lord of the Manor[5]. One wonders how this toll was operated. Even allowing for the fact that the village was small and that there was a fair chance of the ferryman recognising most of its inhabitants, how was it possible to prove that one qualified for the smaller toll? It is recorded that by 1629 the Lord of the Manor was receiving fifteen shillings from the ferry[6] – which is also curious since it is less than the sum mentioned in the Domesday Book.

Several references to Putney are to be found in the accounts of Thomas Cromwell, Earl of Essex. These examples are from 1538:

30 April – Keeper of Moretelacke park, 3s 4d; twelve poor women at Putneth, 4s

16 May – for ferrying at Richmond and Putnethe, 16d

8 July – Poor folks at Putnethe 16s and boat hire to Putnethe and to Chelsey again; 2s 8d[7]

Thomas Cromwell was a local boy who made good. He was born in about 1485. His father was a fuller or a smith. Henry VIII later granted him the Manor of Wimbledon and it must have been rather splendid for the artisan's son to find himself Lord of the Manor in which he was born and to be able to give shillings to poor people.

Cromwell spent many years in the service of Cardinal Wolsey who also enters Putney's history briefly. When the latter fell into the King's disfavour:

> he made him ready to depart with all his gentlemen and yeomen which was no small number. And took his barge at his privy stairs and so went by water unto Putnethe where all his horses waited his coming... When he was with all his train arrived and landed at Putnethe he took his mule and every man his horse, and setting forth not the length of a pair of garden butts he espied a man coming riding empost down the hill in Putnethe town demanding of his footmen who they thought it should be. And they answered again and said that they supposed it should be Sir Harry Norris. And by and by he come to my lord and saluted him and said that the king's majesty had commended him to his grace and willed him to be in any wise of good cheer, for he was as much in his highness' favour as ever he was... But when he heard Mr Norris rehearse all the good and comfortable words of the King, he quickly lighted from his mule all alone as he had been the youngest person amongst us, and incontinent kneeled down in the dirt upon both his knees holding up his hands for joy... and that done he covered again his head and arose and would have mounted his mule, but he could not mount again with such agility as he lighted before where his footmen had as much ado to set him up in the saddle as they could have[8].

Associated with Wolsey and, like Thomas Cromwell, a son of Putney was Nicholas West who was born in about 1461 and is thought to have been the son of a fishmonger. With the Cardinal's help, he became

Bishop of Ely. In about 1533, shortly before his death, he caused a beautiful Chantry Chapel to be built on to St Mary's Church in Putney[9]. The chapel survives and is perhaps the finest thing in the church.

There are many traditions and some documentation relating to visits by Royalty in Tudor times. There is, for example, this curious entry in the calendared documents of the reign of Henry VIII:

The charges of Robin the King's Majesty's spaniel keeper...

14 September (1546)... for hair cloth to rub the spaniels with, and for meat and lodging at Maidenhead and Windsor and at Putney when the King dined at my lord of Hartfordes[10].

Queen Elizabeth was a frequent visitor to Putney. John Lacy was honoured by no fewer than twelve Royal visits[11]. Lacy is reputed to have been a member of the Clothmakers' Company – a rich man. John Lacy's house was a large mansion near the river, west of the High Street. It was called *The Palace* because of its royal associations.

CHAPTER FOUR

Parish and Parks

S trictly Putney did not become a parish as opposed to a chapelry within Wimbledon Parish until about 1860, but for centuries before it was referred to as a parish. The parish included Roehampton, often described as a *hamlet* of Putney.

The parish boundaries relied largely on natural features except on the Heath where the division was a series of straight projections between marking stones. The northern boundary was, of course, the Thames. On the east it was a stream which was later to take on the inglorious name of the Putney Gutter. It ran from the Heath at Tibbet's Corner to the Thames, and still exists although its course is now in an underground drain. Since the viaduct of the District railway line has been built almost on top of most of its course, it has not left many signs of its former route. A dip in Lytton Grove, an access door on the Upper Richmond Road next to East Putney station, and a pipe over the main-line railway cutting are all that serve to remind us of it today. From Tibbet's Corner the boundary extended nearly to the windmill and then turned in a south-westerly direction until it met Beverley Brook which was the boundary right through the area where Richmond Park was enclosed, and on down the hill to the Upper Richmond Road. It followed this road eastwards for some way, then turned north along Dyers Lane and across Putney Lower Common to the Beverley Brook which completes the loop by flowing into the Thames. Boundary stones are to be found on the Heath (one in front of Ross Court, one north of the windmill, and a third where the boundary joins the Beverley Brook) and beating the bounds on this portion of their circuit makes a splendid perambulation over some of the finest portions of the Heath. On the Lower Common boundary markers are to be seen on each side of Queen's Ride. On the Lower Richmond Road is a fine memorial to the days when parish boundaries mattered: this is the cattle keeper's lodge (incorporated in a building of 1913). The duty of the cattle-keeper was to prevent cattle straying between the commons of Barnes and Putney. Right along the Common is a distinct earth mound which is all that remains of a hedge which divided the parishes.

Parish boundaries are not considered very important today, but used to be of vital importance. Each village was surrounded by common lands over which the inhabitants had certain right. These are set out in a document of the nineteenth century:

> ... the freehold and copyhold tenants of the manor of Wimbledon... have enjoyed as of right and without interruption the following rights, viz. (1) a right to have and enjoy the whole of the said Common called Wimbledon Common..., but including Putney Heath and Putney Lower Common, ... open and unenclosed... . (2) a right of pasture upon the said Common...; (3) a right... to cut so much turf, furze, gorse, fern, underwood, pollard, thorns, bushes and brambles, and to dig so much gravel, sand, loam, clay, peat, bog earth and stones as might be required for the purpose of fodder and litter for cattle... and for fuel and other purposes of agriculture and husbandry... and for the reparation of houses and other buildings and hedges and gates... (4) a right to use the said Common for walking, driving, riding, and riding on horseback, and for the enjoyment of air and exercise, and for lawful sports and games at reasonable times, and for amusement and recreation; and (5) other rights, privileges and customs[1].

Clearly when England was still a largely agrarian country the common lands were of vital importance in the economy and way of life of the villages. Parish boundaries had to be guarded against encroachment by neighbouring parishes: to do this the boundaries were beaten at irregular intervals. The clergy and villagers would proceed round the boundary which was maintained as a right of way. Residents of adjoining parishes were *bumped* against the boundary markers to make the place stick in their memories. Apart from those who were bumped, everyone seems to have had a jolly time beating the bounds and the parish provided refreshments afterwards[2]. The parish marker which was to cause the greatest degree of hilarity was that on the roadway in the middle of the bridge because, added to the fact that there was a plentiful supply of strangers to be bumped, there was the pleasure of being able to walk onto the bridge without paying toll[3].

The year 1637 marks the completion of a project which gave modern Putney one of its most splendid legacies, although it was not seen in this light at the time. The project in question was the enclosing of Richmond Park by Charles I. Discussing Richmond Park in a history of Putney is not as strange as it may seem: of the 2,358 acres which form the total, only 69 are in Richmond and 236 were in the old parish of Putney. Much of the area, consisting of waste ground, Crown lands and commons, had been used as a royal hunting ground for many reigns previously. But the arrangement of this land was haphazard and the sport was uncertain.

The King, who was excessively affected to hunting and the sports of the field, had a great desire to make a great park for red as well as fallow deer between Richmond and Hampton Court, where he had large wastes of his own and great parcels of wood, which made it very fit for the use he designed it to: but as some parishes had common in those wastes, so many gentlemen and farmers had good houses and good farms intermingled with those wastes… and without taking in of them into the park, it would not be of the largeness nor for the use proposed. His majesty desired to purchase those lands, and was very willing to buy them upon higher terms than the people could sell them at to anybody else if they had occasion to part with them, and thought it no unreasonable thing upon those terms to expect from his subjects. The major part of the people were in a short time prevailed with, but many very obstinately refused; and a gentleman who had the best estate, with a convenient house and gardens, would by no means part with it; and the King being as earnest to compass it, it made a great noise, as if the King would take away men's estates at his own pleasure. The Bishop of London, who was Treasurer, and the Lord Cottington, Chancellor of the Exchequer, were, from the first entering upon it, very averse from the design, not only for the murmur of the people but because the purchase of the land, and the making a brick wall about so large a parcel of ground (for it is not less than ten or twelve miles about), would cost a greater gum of money than they could easily provide, or that they thought ought to be sacrificed to such an occasion; and the Lord Cottington (who was more solicited by the country people, and heard most of their murmurs) took the business most to heart, and endeavoured by all the ways he could and by frequent importunities to divert his majesty from pursuing it, and put all delays he could well do in the bargains which were to be made, till the King grew very angry with him, and told him he was resolved to go through with it, and had already caused brick to be burned, and much of the wall to be built upon his own land; upon which Cottington thought fit to acquiesce.

The building of the wall before people consented to part with their land or their common looked to them as if by degrees they should be shut out from both, and increased the murmur and noise of the people who were not concerned as well as of them who were, and it was too near London not to be the common discourse[4].

Charles got his way: but it is believed that this project, pushed forward so obstinately and arbitrarily, contributed significantly to his unpopularity. But even he, with his pretensions to absolutism did not try completely to override the inherited rights of the villagers to the common lands which he had enclosed. Rights of way were preserved through the park and doors were provided in the walls at those points where they crossed the parish boundaries so that the ceremony of beating the bounds could be followed without interruption. Parishioners were entitled to collect fallen wood and parish officers could authorise the digging of ground for the maintenance of roads.

After the King was executed, the Commons passed an Act for the sale of Crown lands but Richmond Park was specifically exempted. On 30 June 1649, the House of Commons passed a resolution:

That the City of London have the New Park, in the County of Surrey, settled upon them and their Successors: and that an act be brought to that Purpose.

At the Restoration, the Park returned to the monarchy and it continues as a Royal park to this day. But it was not quite as simple as that. During the reigns of George II and George III there were introduced a series of measures designed to limit entrance to the park and to deny rights of way.

Two court cases ensued. The first was Symons v. Shaw (12 and 13 November 1754) in which the villagers of East Sheen tried to prove a right of way through the park for vehicles and pedestrians. The verdict was given against the villagers – probably because of the poor presentation of their case. The second case, Rex v. Martha Gray (3 April 1758 at Kingston Assizes), was more successful. Right of way for pedestrians was upheld and ladder-stiles were set up at various points along the wall[5].

Under successive reigns the Park has become ever more accessible and organised for the recreational needs of a vast city. There are two golf courses, twenty-four football fields, eleven rugby grounds, one polo ground, and other facilities. But much more than that, it is a huge, splendid, open place in which the city dweller can walk or sit or breathe fresh air or make love, or get lost.

With the creation of the *New Park* Putney gained a part interest in one of London's finest open spaces: but when Royalty had created this magnificent park, it lost interest in its older and smaller one in Putney.

We have tried to trace the gradual development and growth of Putney from its humble beginnings and through the more glamorous Tudor period. The story so far has been only indirectly involved with world affairs. This changed suddenly when, for a brief period, the village was thrust into the forefront of English history.

CHAPTER FIVE

The Putney Debates

F or really I think that the poorest he that is in England hath a life to
live, as the greatest he; and therefore truly, sir, I think it's clear, that
every man that is to live under a government ought first by his own
consent to put himself under that government[1]

The Putney Debates, which represent a turning point in the struggle for
democracy, took place at a time when the Roundheads had already
won the English Civil War. Oliver Cromwell's New Model Army had
bested the Cavaliers and Charles I himself was in custody at Hampton
Court. Officers, rank and file of the Roundhead army argued their case
for a democratic state based on male suffrage, religious toleration,
rights of property and parliamentary reform. Transcripts of the debates
taken by army secretary William Clarke only came to light in the
nineteenth century. These extraordinary discussions remain as vibrant
today as in 1647.

Putney's closeness to Parliament in London and to the King at
Hampton Court, just a few miles away and easily accessible by horse,
coach or boat, attracted the Army in 1647. Putney had experienced
several upheavals as a result of the war. Soldiers had passed through
or been billetted, several times bringing plague with them. The most
important landholder, Sir Thomas Dawes, whose father Sir Abraham
had done extremely well out of the King as a collector of the
customs, was ruined by heavy fines. What Putney's inhabitants
thought of the Army in their midst is not recorded, but they
undoubtedly bitterly resented having soldiers billetted upon them
without payment.

The Army spent 12 weeks in Putney, from 26 August to 17 November.
Officers and soldiers must have been a familiar sight on the streets,
and a great deal of political debate must have taken place in houses
great and small. From 9 September the Army's General Council met
every Thursday in St Mary's.

The Civil War between King and Parliament, i.e. Cavaliers and Roundheads, began in 1642, over issues such as the King's arbitrary powers and his changes to the Church of England. Parliament's forces finally triumphed in 1646. But a political settlement proved elusive, largely because the King played for time while seeking to divide his enemies and raise new forces.

Meanwhile, in 1647, Parliament's attempts to disband the Army provoked it into defiance. The majority in Parliament regarded the Army as a hotbed of religious radicalism, as well as hugely expensive, and therefore a major obstacle to a return to normal peace-time life. The soldiers came to see Parliament as an ungrateful institution which, after they had achieved victory for it, wanted to disband them or send them to fight in Ireland without even granting their arrears of pay or providing indemnity from prosecution for acts committed during the war.

Resistance to disbandment was begun by the rank and file, who elected *agitators* in each regiment and refused to follow those officers who agreed to go to Ireland. In June 1647, Fairfax and Cromwell decided that they could preserve the Army's unity only by joining and leading its opposition to Parliament. The overriding need for unity led to the establishment of the General Council of the Army, consisting both of senior officers and of agitators elected by the rank and file and junior officers in each regiment. This was how ordinary soldiers came to have a voice alongside the Army 'grandees' such as Cromwell. It was in the General Council that the Putney Debates took place.

One of the purposes of the General Council's meetings was to agree peace terms which could be put to the King and Parliament with the support of the whole Army. By October the lack of progress on reform or in negotiations with the King gave rise to increasing discontent and growing distrust of the King and of those negotiating with him. This was reflected in *The Case of the Armie Truly Stated*. An invitation to its authors to explain their concerns in the General Council was followed by the submission of a much more radical paper entitled *An Agreement of the People*. Thus the radical ideas in the *Agreement* came to be discussed in the Debates, which began the following day.

The Civil War was a war of words as well as weapons. For the first time the power of the press became hugely important. The Levellers in particular exploited this way of influencing popular opinion with a flood of polemical pamphlets. The Levellers were the first democratic political movement in modern history, unmatched in any country until the eighteenth century. Their central political idea was that all power originated in the people, who entrusted their elected representatives with as much of it as they chose and who should keep control of their representatives through frequent elections and fundamental laws enshrined in a written constitution. *Leveller.*was a term used by their enemies, implying that they wanted to level all distinctions of rank and property.

The Levellers were a largely London-based civilian movement. They gained significant support in the Army, but most of the soldiers were consistently interested only in the issues which affected them as soldiers. At the time of the Debates the Levellers were only just beginning to become an organised movement, and their main leader, John Lilburne, was imprisoned in the Tower. They seem to have influenced one of the key pamphlets of October 1647, *The Case of the Armie Truly Stated*, and to have written the other, *An Agreement of the People*.

The Putney Debaters were undoubtedly the most extraordinary group of men ever assembled at Putney. Sons of gentlemen sat side by side with shoemakers and button-sellers. Their careers after the Debates varied greatly: some sank into obscurity; others continued in military or naval careers or in other political or religious activity. Seven signed the death warrant of Charles I. Following the Restoration, one (Hugh Peter) was executed, two spent the rest of their lives in prison, and two fled abroad. Some remained true to a set of political or religious principles, whereas others radically changed their views, a few even becoming royalists or Catholics.

One of the most remarkable aspects of the Debates was the participation of ordinary soldiers. Only five spoke (all from cavalry regiments), one declaring himself "but a poor man and unacquainted with the affairs of the Kingdom", but they put their case forcefully. Many officers had radical political or religious views, and it was a senior officer, Colonel Thomas Rainborough, who expressed them most memorably.

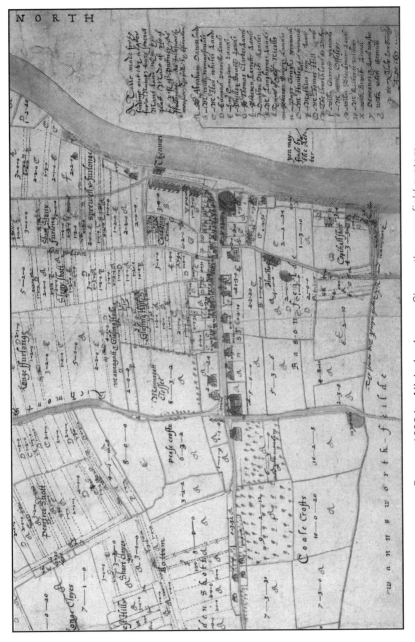

Putney 1636 by Nicholas Lane – Shows the open field system

From June 1647 the Army was united in proposing a more equal distribution of parliamentary seats. *An Agreement of the People* went much further, calling for representation to be proportional to the number of inhabitants, which implied that every inhabitant (or at least every male inhabitant) would have the vote. This sparked the most passionate and fascinating part of the Putney Debates. The Levellers had not entirely thought the idea through, and one of their speakers conceded that apprentices, servants and recipients of charity should be excluded 'because they depend on the will of other men' and so (in the absence of a secret ballot) could not vote freely.

In fact the franchise was not one of the most divisive issues. Clarke's transcript does not record it, but other sources indicate that there was near-unanimous agreement at Putney on extending the vote to "all souldiers and others, if they be not servants or beggars". If implemented this would have transformed the country's political life. It was not until near the end of the nineteenth century that a young historian, Charles Firth, the future regius professor of history in Oxford University, had his attention drawn to a group of manuscripts relating to the English Civil War lying in a cupboard in Worcester College Oxford. He had discovered documents that not only reveal the intimate workings of Cromwell's army at the point when it entered the political arena, but also hitherto unknown aspects of Cromwell himself. Firth edited the manuscripts for the Camden Society (later to become the Royal Historical Society) in 1891 and 1894 and they became known as *The Clarke Papers'* – the work of an army secretary called William Clarke.

On 11 November the King escaped from Hampton Court, and on 17 November Army headquarters left Putney. A Leveller-inspired mutiny was suppressed at Ware.

The ideas in the *Agreement* came closer to being implemented in late 1648, after the Second Civil War, when the Army had purged Parliament, was preparing to try the King and needed a franchise which would not result in a Royalist Parliament. The franchise would have been similar to the one agreed at Putney but with many potential electors excluded on political grounds. However, even a purged House of Commons was not willing to implement this. In 1649 Leveller attempts to stir up mutiny created an irreconcilable gulf between them and the Army, and the Leveller leaders were imprisoned. The time for radical reforms had passed for the time being. But the ideas discussed at Putney would never be forgotten.

An exhibition *The Putney Debates 1647: Cromwell and Democracy 2007 opened in 2007* in St Mary's Church as a monument to celebrate one of the most important events in our constitutional history, and to increase people's understanding of how local heritage plays a crucial role in a nation's history. St Mary's won a Guardian readers' competition in 2006 for the event most needing marking in Britain's radical past, and funding was raised from Heritage Lottery Fund to create the exhibition.

The exhibition at St Mary's includes extracts from the Clarke. transcripts of the Debates, protagonists in the Debates including local firebrand preacher Hugh Peters, an article by Geoffrey Robertson QC on Democracy and Civil Rights, and an audio narrative with extracts from the Debates and audio description of the exhibition. Jack Straw, Tony Benn, Antonia Fraser, Geoffrey Robertson QC and leading historians John Morrill and Quentin Skinner are amongst those who give their views on the importance of the Putney Debates to the formation of democracy in video interviews with Tristram Hunt. **www.putneydebates.com**

CHAPTER SIX
To Build a Bridge

The first project for building a bridge over the Thames at Putney was the subject of a Parliamentary debate on 4 April 1671. The opponents of the scheme were the watermen and the City of London – both of whom had vested interests. The debates make fascinating reading as an exercise in special pleading:

Mr Jones, Member for London; This Bill will question the very being of London; next to the pulling down of the borough of Southwark, nothing can ruin it more. All the correspondences westward, for fuel, and grain, and hay, if this bridge be built, cannot be kept up – The water there is shallow at ebb; the correspondences of London require free passage at all times; and if a bridge, a sculler can scarce pass at low water. It will alter the affairs of waterman, to the King's damage, and the nation's – Thinks the Bill unreasonable and unjust.

Mr Waller;... If ill for Southwark, it is good for this end of the town, where Court and Parliament are. At Paris there are many bridges – At Venice hundreds – We are still obstructing public things. The King cannot hunt, but he must cross the water. He and the whole nation have convenience of it.

Sir Tho. Lee;... This Bill will make the new buildings at this end of the town let the better, and fears the Bill is only for that purpose...

Mr Secretary Trevor;... Passages over rivers are generally convenient; and by the same reason you argue against this bridge, you may argue against London Bridge and the ferries.

Sir William Thompson;... The rents of London Bridge, for the maintenance of it, will be destroyed. This bridge will cause sands and shelves, and have an effect upon the low bridge navigation, and cause the ships to lie as low as Woolwich; it will affect your navigation, your seamen, and your Western barges, who cannot pass at low water –

Would reject the Bill…

Mr Boscawen;… If a bridge at Putney, why not at Lambeth, and more?…

Mr Love;… He hears that it must be of timber, which must be vast, and so hinder the tide, that watermen must stay till it rises. When between the bridges the streams are abated, in time no boat will pass, and the river will be destroyed totally for passage, it being already full of shelves[1].

It hardly needs to be added, after all that, that the bill was rejected – by 67 votes to 54.

But even the vested interests of the City and the watermen and the sheer stupidity displayed in Parliament that day had, eventually, to give way. In 1726 an act was passed "for building a Bridge cross the River of Thames from the Town of Fulham in the County of Middlesex, to the town of Putney in the County of Surrey".

There is a nice irony in the fact that in 1735, when it was proposed to build a bridge at Westminster, the Putney Bridge Company petitioned Parliament not to allow the proposed bridge as it would prejudice their interests[2]!

The old bridge did not occupy the same site as the present structure: it was further east so that at the Putney end the road made a sharp swerve westwards to avoid the church. This curious alignment was probably due to the fact that the designer wished to make use of the sandbank which was postulated in discussing the ferry.

C G Harper gives us an amusing description of the old bridge:

What Londoner worthy of the name does not regret the old crazy; timbered bridge that connected Fulham with Putney? Granted that it was inconveniently narrow, and humped in unexpected places, like a dromedary, conceded that its many and mazy piers obstructed navigation and hindered the tides; allowing every objection against it, old Putney Bridge was infinitely more interesting than the present one of stone which sits so low in the water and offends the eye with its matter-of-fact regularity...[3]

There is some controversy about who was responsible for the design of this curious structure. G W C Green[4] states definitely that it was designed by Sir Joseph Ackworth. But tradition ascribes it to a Mr Cheselden, a surgeon of St. Thomas's and Chelsea Hospital: "...the surgeon of Chelsea Hospital for old soldiers was the right man to build the bridge, because it had so many wooden legs..."[5]

This story seems too good to be true but it appears that for once tradition is correct. On the 2 July 1730 the proprietors of the bridge passed the following resolution:

> Resolved, as the bridge is built entirely according to a scheme and principles laid down by Mr Cheselden, and as he has been very serviceable in directing the execution of the same, that the thanks of the proprietors be given to him... they being of opinion that no timber bridge can be built in a more substantial and commodious manner than that which is now erected[6].

The bridge was some 790 feet long and had openings beneath for river traffic. The centre opening was named *Walpole's Lock* in honour of Sir Robert Walpole who did much to ease the passage of the bill through Parliament[7]. This opening was only thirty feet wide and so at a later date the centre spans were removed and a single iron span was inserted in their place. This provided an opening seventy feet wide and also gave an additional river height, or headway, of three feet[8].

A toll was due from those who used the bridge. The Act lays down the following scale of charges:

> For every Coach, Chariot, Berlin, Chaise, Chair or Calash, drawn by Six or more horses, the Sum of Two Shillings.
>
> For every Coach, Chariot, Berlin. . . drawn by Four horses, the Sum of One Shilling and Six Pence.
>
> For every Coach, Chariot, Berlin. . . drawn by less than four horses, the

Sum of One Shilling.

For every Waggon, Wain, Dray, Carr, Cart or Carriage, drawn by four or more horses or Oxen, the Sum of One Shilling and Six Pence; and by less than four horses or Oxen, the Sum of One Shilling.

For every horse, Mule or Ass, laden or unladen, and not drawing, the Sum of Two Pence.

For every foot Passenger on Sundays, one Penny; and on every other Day, One halfpenny.

For every drove of Oxen neat Cattle, the Sum of Twelve Pence per Score; and after that Rate for any greater or less number.

For every drove of Calves, Hogs, Sheep, or Lambs, the Sum of Six Pence per Score; and after that Rate for a greater or less Number.

Which said respective Sums of Money shall and may be demanded and taken in the Name of Pontage, or as a Toll or Duty; and the Monies to be received, as aforesaid, and all other Monies to be received by Authority of this Act.

It will have been noticed that the toll was doubled on Sundays. The extra money so raised was divided annually between the widows and children of poor watermen as a recompense for the watermen's Sunday ferry rendered worthless by the bridge… Lysons tells us that the sum amounted to about £62; this gives an idea of the volume of traffic using the bridge – a simple calculation shows that about 600 pedestrians must have crossed it every Sunday.

The toll gate on the Fulham side straddled the roadway arch fashion, and the arch was so low that it was a considerable danger to outside passengers on the stage coaches[9]. From old maps it seems that the toll house on the Putney side was built into the angle between the roadway and the church, the toll-keepers were provided with impressive-looking gowns and staves. The staves were not for decoration. Thieves and highwaymen visited the toll houses frequently and country waggoners objected to having to pay toll: after all, London

Bridge provided a free crossing so why not this one? Bells were hung from the toll houses so that the toll-keepers could call on each other's assistance in times of trouble[10].

But the bridge had a monopoly since it provided the only dry crossing between London and Kingston. Within two years of its construction the tolls were producing an income of £1,500 per annum. In 1792 Lysons wrote"... it is now supposed to be nearly double that sum and constantly increasing"[11].

CHAPTER SEVEN
Highways, Travellers and Highwaymen

As road traffic grew in the seventeenth and eighteenth centuries, the two major routes through Putney parish became increasingly important. The road up West Hill and across Putney Heath towards Kingston (the modern A3) was the main route for travellers from London to Portsmouth. This road was used by the Portsmouth stage-coaches, which began in the 1650s and flourished in the late eighteenth and nineteenth centuries before being superseded by railways. The route from London across Putney Bridge and on to Richmond and Kingston was more important to Putney itself, bringing travellers and their vehicles and providing trade for innkeepers, blacksmiths and others.

Putney sometimes made a definite effort to maintain its roads. In 1656 thirteen parishioners petitioned the Lord Protector (Oliver Cromwell):

> On the humble petition of divers parishioners of Putney in the County of Surrey whose names are subscribed showing that in pursuance of the Ordinance of his Highness and the Counsell for amending and retaining highways, the said parishioners have raysed and expended in the two years last past Considerable somes of money and do find that the high street of the said towne being a very great road and of great length and breadth cannot be sufficiently made by the ordinary way of gravelling the same their whole cost therein being hitherto lost for remedy whereof as well for the general good as for their own Convenience they are willing to undergo the charge of paving the said high street. Ordered by His Highness the Lord Protector and his Counsell that the monies risen and to be raised by the assessments within the said parish by vertue of the said ordinance shall be employed upon the said pavement and other necessary worke appertaining to the said High Waye by the Surveyor thereof for the tyme being until the undertaking of the said worke be satisfyed[1].

Another relatively well-maintained road, after it was turnpiked in 1718, was the A3. In 1820 Sir Richard Phillips wrote that:

> A pedestrian like the writer could not avoid feeling grateful to the constructor of this piece of road, for its beautiful and spacious causeway, which extends from the village of Wandsworth to Putney Heath. It is in most parts seven feet wide, and it doubtless owes much of its hardness, smoothness and dryness to its declining position, which causes the water to run off...[2]

Some record has survived of those who used the roads. For example, the cash books of the Putney Bridge toll collectors record that "on 8 February 1740 there passed over the bridge 12 six-horse coaches, three four-horse coaches, 24 coaches drawn by fewer than four horses, 334 horses, mules and asses, 15 hogs and 1052 foot passengers."[3] The Putney churchwardens' accounts record poor travellers who received charity as they passed through. In April 1732-March 1733, when the accounts are particularly full, there were: " 476 sailors, 99 other men, 46 'bigbellyed' (i.e. pregnant) women, 89 other women and at least 75 children, including '19 slaves out of Turkey some thire toungs cutt out' and 'a bigbelly'd woman for Guilford like to fall in peices'".[4]

Many of the public houses we know today date back to the seventeenth and eighteenth centuries. The oldest are the Fox (originally the Anchor) and the Walkabout (originally the White Lion), both of which existed by 1617, though their current buildings are much later. The latter is the last survivor of a group of inns which stood just opposite the ferry landing. The public houses with the oldest buildings are the Green Man, built in about 1700, and the King's Head in Roehampton, possibly dating from the1670s. Other long-established public houses are the Duke's Head (1714) and the Half Moon (1721). Eight of the public house licensed in 1786 survive today – the Duke's Head, the Fox, the Green Man, the Half Moon, the Spotted Horse, the Star and Garter, the Walkabout and, in Roehampton, the Angel.

Among the more intriguing figures from Putney's past are the highwaymen. Their frequent operation in this area is a fine testimony to Putney's importance as a thoroughfare, as well as the value to

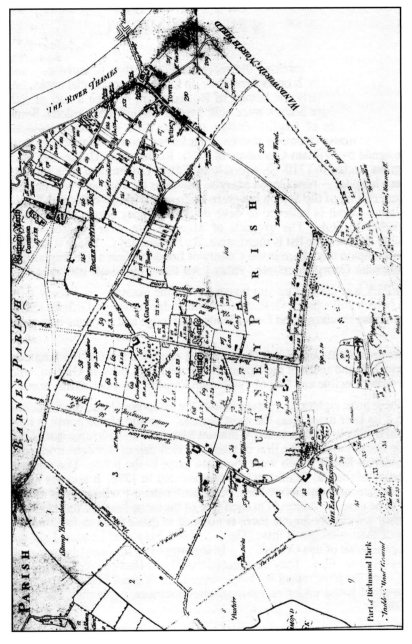

Putney 1787 by John Corris – Plan of Putney Parish

highwaymen of uninhabited areas such as Putney Heath. We read for example of Augustine Bird who was indicted in 1740 for robbing Simon Hughes in the King's Highway on Putney Heath[5]. And the General Advertiser of Wednesday 29 August 1750 notes that:

> On Monday evening a Highwayman was taken up at the White Lyon at Putney, and committed to the New Goal (sic) in Southwark, for robbing – Clarke, Esq.; on Friday last; which was the second time of his robbing that Gentleman.

A little lower down on the same page, we read that:

> On Monday last a Man was taken in a chaise with a Lady on Putney-Bridge, charged with committing several Robberies lately near Camberwell, Dulwich, etc.

The most notorious of the highwaymen was Louis Jeremiah Abershaw, usually known as *Jerry Abershaw*. He was the terror of the roads in this area. He had his headquarters in the Bald-Faced Stag – on the Kingston Road, near where the Putney Vale Cemetery is today. In 1795 he shot dead a constable sent to arrest him in Southwark. He was hanged on Kennington Common and his body was displayed on the Heath (clearly the origin of the story that there was a gibbet on Putney Heath).

Tibbet's Corner, at the top of Putney Hill, has given rise to wild speculation. It is commonly believed that the place was named after a highwayman who operated in the area. Another suggestion is that *Tibbet* is a corruption of *Gibbet* – which fits in nicely with the highwayman theory. Both theories are wrong, however. Tibbet was the name of the footman of the second Countess Spencer. He lived in the lodge previously situated at the entrance to Wimbledon Park.[6]

CHAPTER EIGHT

Roehampton, 15th to 21st Century

Roehampton is a story of people and property – Lords, ladies, commoners, politicians and prime ministers, with homes including palatial mansions and Corbusier inspired towers. Roehampton emerged from being a small hamlet, originally situated in Roehampton Lane by the edge of Putney Heath to the most exclusive village in England.

People developed and changed Roehampton, but as they passed on, many buildings merely adapted their purpose, and survived to fulfil a continuing destiny in a different form. By 1497 there were 14 houses, and by 1617 Roehampton had grown to a village of 33 houses.

Although some sources credit the development of Roehampton to the Huguenots, Wandsworth did not become a Huguenot stronghold until the 1680s. However Roehampton was transformed by the Huguenot David Papillon who purchased a house there in 1620.

Papillion developed several major houses not least the original Roehampton Great House and Elm Grove. Throughout the 17th century grand houses were built in Roehampton and by 1670 the hamlet had doubled in size to 59 dwellings inhabited by 350 souls and now boasted two inns, the Kings Head and the Angel. Both became prominent in today's village. But more development was to come.

Roehampton Great House was from 1648-75 the home of Christiana Countess of Devonshire who employed as both her children's and then her grandchildren's tutor the philosopher Thomas Hobbes. Similarly the Gibbon family in Putney employed the theologian William Law. The founders of Methodism, the Wesley brothers once walked from Oxford to meet with Law.

The Countess stayed loyal to the Royalist cause throughout the Civil War and was rewarded by several visits by Charles the Second and his brother James, Duke of York. They also enjoyed swimming at Putney.

Subsequently the Great House was pulled down and rebuilt in 1777 by Joshua Vanneck, Lord Huntingfield, becoming later known as Grove House, part of the renowned Froebel Institute, and now part of Roehampton University.

Meanwhile another magnificent, still surviving house, confusingly called *Roehampton House* had been built on the opposite side of Roehampton Lane in 1712 by Thomas Archer. It is considered one of the finest baroque buildings in the country. Later it became a central part of Queen Mary's Hospital and has now been transformed again into exclusive apartments as part of an interesting 600 home estate.

Roehampton's large and often gracious houses with their accompanying estates became the country residences of aristocrats, politicians and successful businessmen who during the week worked in the City of London. Part of the attraction of having a country residence was the appalling levels of disease, smell and physical corruption which existed in the crowded City.

All the country villages around London including Dulwich, Streatham, Battersea, Chelsea and Putney enjoyed a golden period between the rise of the metropolis in the 17th century and the coming of the railway in the 19th century.

In 1726 Daniel Defoe wrote in his Tour of Great Britain about Roehampton. "These are all houses of retreat, gentlemen's summer houses, or citizens' country houses; whither they retire from the hurries of business."

Of all the great eighteenth century houses the Fireproof House (or *Wildcroft* to give it its later name) was the most curious. The site of this house is now occupied by blocks of flats called Wildcroft Manor. Two structures associated with the house remain. The first of these is a rich pair of wrought-iron gates (on Wildcroft Road) which were the main gates to the house. The other is the Hartley Memorial Obelisk which was erected in 1776. On each face of the stone base are inscriptions. "The… Lord Mayor of London Laid the Foundation Stone of this Obelisk… In memory of an Invention for securing buildings Against Fire." They also record that David Hartley received £2,500 reward from the government for his invention. Sir Richard Phillips, who saw the fire-proof house explains Hartley's invention:

> …When I saw it, (it) was filled with workmen who were converting it into a tasteful mansion, adding wings to it, throwing out veranders, and destroying every vestige of its original purpose. One of the workmen shewed me the chamber in which in 1774, the King and Queen took their breakfast, while, in the room beneath, fires were lighted on the floor, and various inflammable materials were ignited, to prove that the rooms above were fireproof. The alterations making at the moment enabled me to comprehend the whole of Mr Hartley's system. Parts of the floors having been taken up, it appeared that they were double, and that his contrivance consisted in interposing between the two boards, sheets of laminated iron or copper[1].

Close to the obelisk is a public house known as The Telegraph, which commemorates the signal station set up here in 1796[2]. The Admiralty set up four signal chains between London and the ports of Deal, Yarmouth, Portsmouth and Plymouth. The station at Putney was part of the line to Portsmouth and Plymouth (a shared line which divided into two on the South Downs at Beacon Hill). They were put up since the war with Revolutionary France had greatly increased the need for more dependable and rapid communications with the naval ports.

> After about twenty years' experience, they calculate on about two hundred days on which signals can be transmitted throughout the day; about sixty others on which they can pass only part of the day, or at particular stations; and about one hundred days in which few of the stations can see the others… The station in question is generally rendered useless during easterly winds by the smoke of London, which fills the valley of the Thames between this spot and Chelsea Hospital…[3]

One member of the Putney station, seaman Wood, left an account of the station to a former head of the Putney Library. He explained what happened when smoke did obscure the station at Chelsea Hospital: the message was given to a local gardener who ran down the hill, through the "huddling village High Street, over the bridge to Fulham village and so along the King's Road through the fields to Chelsea." For running this marathon in a specified time, he received a shilling[4]. (NB In the late summer of 1818 John Constable made the pencil sketches of the signal station and of Bristol House on Putney Heath which are in the Fitzwilliam Museum, Cambridge. A tinted drawing of Bristol House, derived from the sketch, is in the Victoria & Albert Museum.)

Papillon's other major building, Elm Grove, was situated where Digby Stuart College is today. Rebuilt in 1795, it was occupied by the Dutch Jewish banker Benjamin Goldsmid who prospered financing the Napoleonic Wars. He entertained on an extravagant scale, rather in the style of the ultra successful today with guest lists reading as a Who's Who of the time including Nelson and even George III. The unfortunate Benjamin suffered from depression and committed suicide. His brother Abraham also a banker, who tried to save Emma Hamilton from bankruptcy, after a fall in the market, also committed suicide.

Lord Chief Justice Edward Law then acquired Elm Grove, as magnificent as a small palace. It, was inherited by his son who later became a dramatically unsuccessful Governor General of India in the 1840s but was also created first Earl of Ellenborough. In 1850 it was the first Roehampton house to pass into institutional use as a convent school with the Order of the Sacred Heart. It was bombed in 1941, subsequently demolished and the site became part of Roehampton University.

Two surviving houses date from the end of the 18th century; Manresa and Mount Clare. Manresa was built for the Earl of Bessborough. His architect Sir William Chambers also built the splendid Somerset House on the Strand. Bessborough's son married Henrietta Spencer, the vivacious, equally socially successful sister of Georgina Duchess of Devonshire. Henrietta kept an open house and entertained her lovers in Roehampton. One failed suitor was the future George IV. Her

continued on page 57

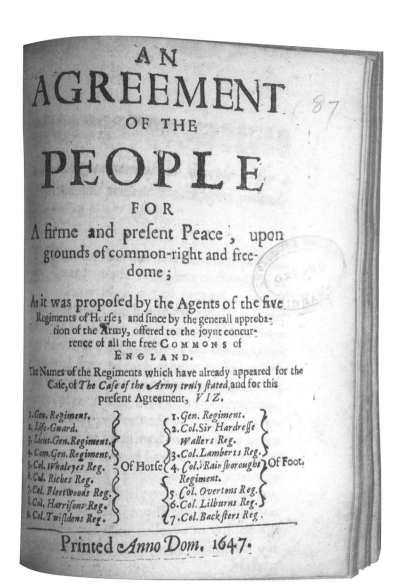

AN
AGREEMENT

OF THE

PEOPLE

FOR

A firme and prefent Peace, upon
grounds of common-right and free-
dome;

As it was propofed by the Agents of the five
Regiments of Horfe; and fince by the generall approba-
tion of the Army, offered to the joynt concur-
rence of all the free COMMONS of
ENGLAND.

The Names of the Regiments which have already appeared for the
Cafe, of *The Cafe of the Army truly ftated*, and for this
prefent Agreement, *VIZ*.

1. Gen. Regiment.		1. Gen. Regiment.
2. Life-Guard.		2. Col. Sir Hardreffe
3. Lieut.Gen. Regiment.		Wallers Reg.
4. Com.Gen. Regiment.		3. Col. Lamberts Reg.
5. Col. Whaleyes Reg.	Of Horfe	4. Col. Rainfboroughs Of Foot.
6. Col. Riches Reg.		Regiment.
7. Col. FleetWoods Reg.		5. Col. Overtons Reg.
8. Col. Harrifons Reg.		6. Col. Lilburns Reg.
9. Col. Twifdens Reg.		7. Col. Backfters Reg.

Printed *Anno Dom.* 1647.

The Agreement of the People

Small flint hand-axe from Dover House Road

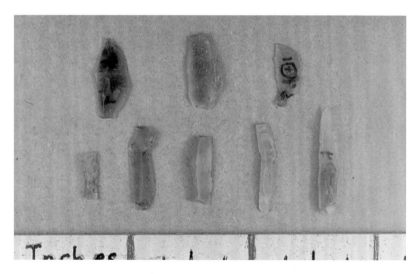

Mesolithic flint microliths from Sefton Street
(characteristic of a late stage in the period)

Pillbox, Putney Bridge Station

The Old Putney Bridge in 1880 – Long before global warming the Thames was often ice bound. Frost fairs were regularly held on the Thames. Between 1400 and 1814 the Thames was completely frozen over 24 times.

*Last pictures of the old **Putney Bridge and Aqueduct 1884** – The aqueduct became the course of the present Putney Bridge built by Sir Joseph Bazelgette and opened in 1886.*

Winchester House, Putney Embankment

Parkstead, Roehampton University, formerly Manresa House

Putney Bridge Toll House 1879 – Tolls were abolished a year later. The pedestrian toll on the old Putney Bridge was a half pence on weekdays and one penny (.5p) at weekends. The old Bridge was built in 1729 and revenue rose from £2500 in 1740 to £6700 in 1810.

Putney Embankment 1895 – Victorians promenading on the new protected tow path. Because of its semi rural, riverside status, Putney was a holiday destination until the First World War.

Mount Clare, Roehampton, University

Alton Estate, Roehampton

Putney High Street 1880 – Flooding was common until the new Bridge and river walls were built in 1886. Note derricks – a sign of a very active river trade to and from Putney Wharf.

Putney High Street 1936 – Putney looking like every other provincial High Street with its unique blend of local shops.

Roehampton House once part of Queen Mary Hospital, Roehampton

WANDSWORTH COUNCIL

CLEMENT RICHARD
ATTLEE
1883 - 1967

1st EARL ATTLEE

Labour Party Leader 1935 - 1955
Deputy Prime Minister 1942 - 1945
Prime Minister 1945 - 1951
Born and raised in a house
on this site

2009

Gavin
EWART
1916 - 1995
Noted Poet
FRSL
Lived at
Kenilworth Court

THE PUTNEY SOCIETY

VII
VI
V
VIII
IX
X XI XII I II III
IV
MM
TIME LIKE
AN EVER
ROLLING
STREAM

Lord Hugh
JENKINS
1908 - 2004
Putney MP 1964 - 1979
Minister for the Arts

Lived at
Kenilworth Court

THE PUTNEY SOCIETY

NORMAN
PARKINSON CBE
1913 - 1990
PHOTOGRAPHER
Lived here
1919 - 1936

THE PUTNEY SOCIETY

*Timber fish trap or fish weir on the Putney foreshore
at low tide March 2009*

continued from page 40

daughter Caroline Lamb was brought up in Roehampton. Caroline married Queen Victoria's first Prime Minster Lord Melbourne and had a scandalous affair with Lord Byron

In the 1850's Manresa became the home of the Jesuit Order in UK, who also contributed St Josephs Church to Roehampton in 1878. The poet Gerard Manley Hopkins studied at this noted Jesuit seminary. In the 1960s with the compulsory purchase of a major part of the Manresa estate in order to provide land for the development of the Alton estate, the Jesuits sold Manresa to what would become Roehampton University and it was renamed as Parkstead House.

Mount Clare was built in 1773 for Clive of India's faithful cousin *Honest George Clive*, and is now a valued part of Roehampton University, as is Downshire House on Roehampton Lane.

Two other, since lost, houses also had famous connections. Clarence Lodge (in the Bank of England grounds) was once associated with the Duke of Clarence (before he became William IV), although he never took up residence there, and his long standing mistress, the actress Mrs. Jordan. They were a devoted couple and had ten children. Their relationship ended when the Royal family insisted he became a married man in 1810.

Bowling Green House, on the old Portsmouth Road was the final home of that most noted of Prime Ministers, William Pitt, from 1804 until his death in 1806. The last resident of the house was master potter Henry Doulton. In 1933 the house came down to become Bowling Green Close.

The early 1900s continued to see a slow expansion of housing around an attractive village centre with all that was required for its local community. Roehampton Village had retained something of its rustic charm, best exemplified by the King's Head Inn, at the foot of the High Street and the Montague Arms in Medfield Street.

A splendid old watering trough for Victorian carriages still exists at the junction of Medfield Street and Roehampton Lane. It was originally modeled on a tomb seen in Italy, and was donated by Yolande Stephens owner of Roehampton Grove at the time.

The wartime period of '39 –'45 is well remembered by Martin Hime, a Roehampton resident since 1928, he and others emphasised the community spirit which inspired the way of life at that time. Adversity brought out the best in a village whose members excelled in going out of their way to help one another.

During the First World War, Gifford House and Roehampton House (which was renamed Queen Mary's) had become hospitals. Queen Mary's played a major role in the Second World War, providing a rehabilitation centre for those with loss of limbs, many of whom would be seen walking through the village in their distinctive blue uniforms.

Not to be overlooked are some 20th century residents with a fine thespian background, Vivienne Leigh and Maureen O'Sullivan were educated at the Sacred Heart Convent on Roehampton Lane. Margaret Lockwood was a long term resident of Fairacres, an immaculate 1930's development on the Lane which replaced Lower Grove House.

And Jack Hawkins, the typically British actor, and an ardent supporter of the Kings Head, lived on the edge of the village in Westmead.

In sharp contrast, in the early 1900s the risqué writer Frank Harris twice lived in Roehampton with his extremely young wife-to-be, Nellie O'Hara; at that time Harris said that Roehampton and the French Riviera were his favourite places in the world.

Lord Hailsham of St Marylebone,(1907-2001) Lord Chancellor 1970-74 and 1979-87, lawyer and politician who held ministerial positions under Eden and MacMillan, lived in Heathfield Gardens for many years.

Dramatic change came to Roehampton after the war, when the London County Council built the massive Alton East and West Estates of the 1950's. It is, in reality, two housing estates. Alton East was created in the early 1950s and provided 744 dwellings on 28 acres; Alton West was formed later in the decade and provided 1867 dwellings on 100 acres. On Alton West, the LCC essentially retained the Georgian landscape and placed within it five ultra modern slab blocks, inspired by Le Corbusier's Unité d'Habitation, and now listed buildings by English Heritage.

While this change swept away a number of fine houses, it was seen as providing much needed better quality housing for many from the deprivation of inner London boroughs. At the same time others remained in a different form. Examples not already mentioned are Templeton House, headquarters of the Froebel Institute, but also perfect to hire as an events location, and the well known Priory Clinic, both on Priory Lane. Downshire House became part of the University of Greenwich.

In addition the New Millennium has seen the establishment of Roehampton University in 2004. It is a small, friendly community based on four colleges with a distinguished history dating back to the 1840s, particularly in the field of Childhood Studies and Education, and which were also among the first in the country to admit women in higher education.

Whitelands College, Froebel, Digby Stuart and Southlands have combined to create a splendid campus in the historic buildings Parkstead, Grove House and Mount Clare together with an exciting new complex on Roehampton Lane. The University has upwards of 8000 students and 1500 staff. The Faculty has a broad range of expertise across the arts and humanities, social, human and life sciences, while maintaining its noted strength in education.

At the same time the old hospital site has seen the creation of both a new modern Queen Mary's Hospital, together with a major development of 600 new homes. Another new arrival has been the Headquarters of UK's tennis ruling body, the LTA, on Priory Lane, and there is the promise of a regenerated Roehampton centre on Danebury Avenue.

Even so, with all the change in Roehampton and the long gone departure of originating builders, Roehampton has retained a large number of fine historic buildings to remind us of its history.

CHAPTER NINE

Growth Begins

In 1836 St Mary's church was rebuilt. The cost of this work was defrayed by a rate on the parishioners added to by voluntary subscriptions and a grant of £430 from the incorporated Society which enable the number of free sittings to be increased to 400[1]. The architect was Edward Lapidge and the work was executed in stock bricks. Elements of a previous rebuilding (of about 1450) were incorporated, notably the tower and Bishop West's chapel was moved from the south to the north side[2]. The parts of the medieval church which survive today (following the 1973 arson attack on the church) are the tower, some of the nave arcading (mid 15th century) and the Bishop West Chapel built in the early 16th century.

As part of the 1836 rebuilding, the six bells were recast and two more were added[3]. The bells have not always been appreciated:

> And now I live in Putney just within the sound of the river by the bridge, and day by day, week in, week out, from years end to years end do one or other of these two peals of wretched cracked unmusical old bells keep going! If All Saints is not echoing out over the sound-carrying water, St. Mary's is doing her best to make morning, noon and night hideous[4].

Putney has retained much of its identity as a village to this day. Edward Carter has this to say about the influence of suburban railways on the urban fabric:

> During the nineteenth century steam trains provided the only means of suburban commuting, and the fact of their existence contributed largely to a suburban growth. A steam train takes a long time to accelerate and draw up, so that for economy of operation the stations had to be fairly widely spaced. The urban units whose growth was stimulated by the railways remained well separated and retained their identity. In each place the station, generally placed as near the town centre as the town authorities would allow, became a social focus...[5]

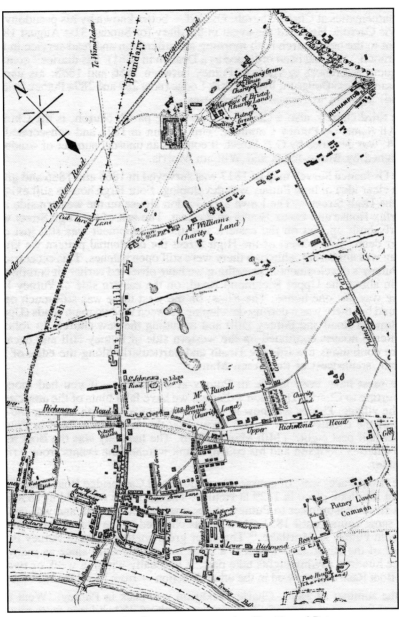

Putney 1859 – *From a report on the Charities of Putney*

The Richmond and West-End Junction Railway Company was formed to build a line from Richmond to the South-Western Railway Company's junction at Battersea (now known as Clapham Junction). An Act was obtained to this end in 1845 and the construction of the six mile line (with stations at Wandsworth, Putney, Barnes and Mortlake), was completed with nine months and at a cost of £170,000[6]. The line was opened on 27 July 1846; the London and South Western Railway bought out the Richmond Company a year later[7].

The station at Putney was not the one we know today. It used to be a Gothic fantasy rather like Barnes Station. Our more workmanlike station dates from 1886 when the railway cutting was widened to admit the doubling of the lines.

If we look at the growth of the parish between 1800 and 1870[8], we notice a sudden upward surge:

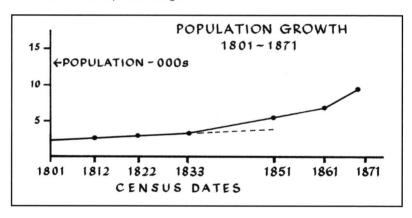

This increase is typical of the growth of London at the time, and maybe helped by the building of the first railway connection.

Demonstrative of the growth of the village is the provision of new churches and burial grounds in Putney. The first relief cemetery to the parish churchyard was built on the Upper Richmond Road in 1763[9] and still as The Putney Old Burial Ground forms a charming and unexpected oasis of calm with some attractive old tombs.

Holy Trinity Church in Roehampton was built in 1898, with a superb spire, almost visible from Richmond, to the design of Fellowes Prynne. It replaced an earlier church of 1842 designed by Benjamin Ferrey. This had become a chapelry church when Putney parish was divided into two parts in 1845. Ferrey's church remained disused until it was demolished in 1928.

The division was equal neither in terms of population nor area. The area of the new parish was 1,239 acres, while that of Putney was 996 acres. But in terms of population the bias was strongly on the other side: the population of Roehampton was 1,497, while the older parish had 7,942 inhabitants.

The Church of England acquired three additional churches in Putney and c. 1860 Putney finally became a separate parish in its own right.

The church of St John the Evangelist was consecrated in 1859. One person who visited the church after the consecration was Charles Lutwidge Dodgson, lecturer in mathematics at Christ Church, Oxford – better known by his pseudonym, Lewis Carroll. He noted the event in his diary for Sunday 31 August 1862: "went to the new church both morning and afternoon and read service in the afternoon." (He had been ordained as a Deacon in 1861.) His diaries[10] contain frequent references to visits to Putney between 1856 and 1868: his uncle, Hassard Hume Dodgson, lived at Park Lodge (now 289 and 289a Putney Bridge Road) adjacent to Dawes's Almshouses. In 1977 the church was sold to the Polish RC community.

The third church is the Church of All Saints on Putney Common. This, begun in 1872 and consecrated in 1874, was designed by G E Street. It contains an unusual number of windows designed by Burne-Jones and William Morris.

The history of the eventual establishment of the Catholic church of Our Lady of Compassion and Saint Simon Stock in Hazlewell Road in 1906 is a testament to the persistence and faith of the Catholic community in Putney. When Henry VIII broke with Rome, in 1543 the Catholic religion survived in hiding until the Reform Act of 1829, supported by those Catholics who were wealthy enough to pay fines and obtain the services of a Priest. Putney was no exception. Under James I a Catholic priest said Mass and ran a school in Putney.

In 1902 The Rev Collinson was appointed as the first Catholic priest for Putney and started his mission with a congregation of 12 in a stable in Coopers Arms Lane rented from The Methodists. The wealthy Leader family who owned a large villa on Putney Hill, now called Lower Park House, as well as land down to the Thames, gave the public Leaders Gardens. John Temple Leader and his descendent Lady Agatha Westbury were instrumental in helping with land for a new Catholic church – the 'Iron church' to be built close to St Simons 1903-6.

St Simons itself was built in 1906 funded by many sources including benefits at The Assembly Rooms. It was consecrated in 1942. During the Second World War in 1944 the Priests' House was gutted, and was rebuilt. Rev Richard Quinlan has been Priest since 1981 presiding over a congregation of 3000, and working ecumenically with all churches in Putney, particularly St Mary's.

The Ordnance Survey map of 1866 and gives us a clear idea of how Putney was developing. Four large houses still existed on the High Street – The Lawn and Gordon House on the western side and Fairfax House and Essex House on the east. The rest of the High Street was nearly built up, but on the eastern side the development was still just one layer deep. To the west of the High Street the residential pattern we know today was appearing, although there were still open patches. On the eastern side of Putney Hill there was just one house, The Elms; on the west there was still much open ground but there was a density developing between the two main roads (Upper Richmond Road and Putney Hill) and including the new church, St John's. Scattered houses continued up the western side of Putney Hill and became more continuous towards the Heath and particularly along the edge of the Heath, south-west of the Green Man.

Life must have been idyllic in Putney at that time – if you had money. Reverting to Charles Dodgson's diaries, we have faint hints of the attractions of the village. Putney was now in rapid communication with London and the rest of the country – "…left Oxford by the 4.40 and arrived in Putney about half past eight." (14 March 1856). The next day

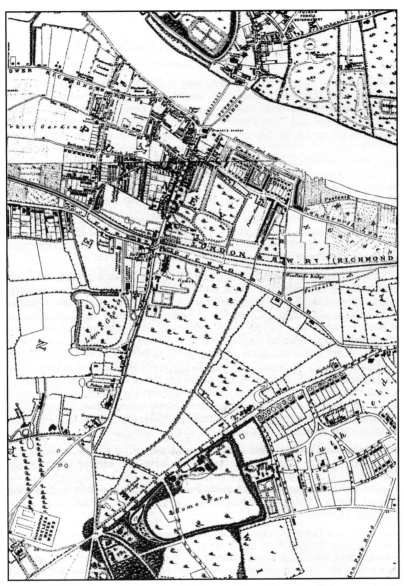

Putney 1862 – *From the Stanford's Library Map of London. This map clearly shows the position of Lime Grove where Edward Gibbon lived and the extensive fields surrounding Putney Hill.*

was the Boat Race and Charles Dodgson and his cousin Frank watched the events from a river steamer.

The *Boat Race* was, of course, the Oxford and Cambridge Boat Race. This event first took place in 1829 at Henley. The next race was held in 1836 and was from Westminster to Putney. It became an annual event and was run on the same course until 1851 when it was changed to the present one, which is from Putney to Mortlake[11]. The other great boating event at Putney is the Head of the River race which is a most impressive sight since as many as three hundred rowing eights take part. It is usually within a week or two of the Boat Race but is rowed in the other direction – from Mortlake to Putney[12].

In the summer of 1856, Charles Dodgson was back in Putney: "Went to a school feast given in the Bullars' garden – about 250 children were present and a number of visitors." (11 June)

The Bullars lived in Fairfax House and could be counted as neighbours of the Dodgsons since their extensive gardens adjoined. The following day "…a miscellaneous sort of party began about three: the day was

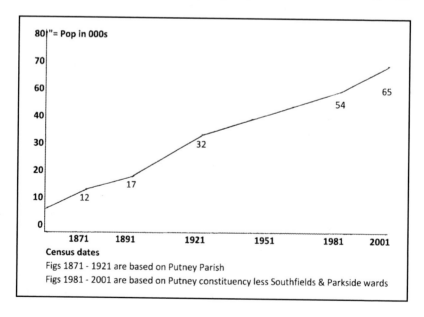

80|" = Pop in 000s

Census dates
Figs 1871 - 1921 are based on Putney Parish
Figs 1981 - 2001 are based on Putney constituency less Southfields & Parkside wards

to have been spent in haymaking but turned out too rainy..."
Haymaking is not something which one would now expect to indulge
in Putney, but the Dodgsons' garden was nearly nine acres in extent
and Putney still had much of the appearance of a country village.

Most of Putney grew up at the end of the nineteenth century. Putney
as we know it is basically a Victorian body on a skeleton which was
fashioned in medieval times or even earlier. The development did not,
of course, take place all at once. There were stages in the spread of
the village and these stages are reflected in the styles of the buildings
which appeared.

Putney's growth over the 50 years up to 1921 can be illustrated by
another graph from the census figures (to the same scale as the
previous one):

But in spite of this, Putney must still have been comparatively open.
We have this description of Putney Hill from a guide book of 1903:

> ...a few new streets are being pushed into the fields, which are,
> however, still continuous to the westward, the limit of building being
> apparently reached for a time in that direction...[13]

The underground railway had a less obvious impact on the expansion
of the village than had the main-line railway. The main-line service had
provided communication where none had existed before: the
underground service provided increased mobility and made Putney
more accessible from a wider range of places. This is illustrated in the
following reminiscence of the conditions of about 1870:

> In my early days at Putney... the only ways of getting from Kensington
> or Hammersmith to Putney were a) to walk; b) to take a cab but, as we
> were beyond the radius, cabmen could make their own terms which
> were not less than five shillings, with a reminder of sixpence extra for
> Putney Bridge toll on week days and a shilling on Sundays; c) to take a
> train at Addison Road and change at Clapham Junction[14].

In 1921 the Dover House Estate was established by the LCC on the
site once occupied by Putney Park. This increased the population of

the area considerably, and in 1923 St Margaret's was elevated to the status of a parish church, the parish being mostly taken from the older parish of Putney but including portions of the parishes of Barnes and Roehampton. The church, the axis of which is north-south instead of the usual east-west, was considerably extended to the north in 1925-6.

In spite of the great expansion we have recorded, Putney and Roehampton were still comparatively wide open in the early decades of the twentieth century. In 1921 the population per acre of the combined parishes was 13 which was one of the very lowest of all London's parishes (excepting the City parishes which had at that time hardly any residential component). Southfields, Putney's neighbour on the south-east, affords a comparison: here the density per acre is 29 – and most of Southfields has the air of a spacious garden suburb. At the same time many thousands of London's poor were living in appalling slum conditions. Putney seemed an obvious choice for a major housing programme. The Dover House Estate was one result of this. Most of the others are later, dating from the 1950s. The huge estates along the northern and eastern edge of Putney Heath date from this time and there are many other, smaller estates, for example the Kersfield Estate between Lytton Grove and Kersfield Road (late 1950s). Here four private houses gave way to 100 dwellings at a density of 70 people per acre.

CHAPTER TEN

Saving the Commons

In the middle of the nineteenth century Putney nearly lost one of its finest possessions – the Heath. The first public move in what was to turn into a protracted battle was that John Poyntz Spencer, the fifth Earl Spencer, the Lord of the Manor of Wimbledon convened a public meeting on the 11 November 1864 in Wimbledon. He explained his scheme for the "protection and improvement" of the common lands which comprise Putney Heath, Wimbledon Common and Wandsworth West Common. He proposed to introduce a bill into Parliament to enable him to enclose a portion of the Common and to develop it as a park. It was to be drained, walled and landscaped. To defray the expenses of this work and also to pay compensation to those whom he considered had rights over the Common (and it appears that he himself, as Lord of the Manor, was one of those who was due to receive compensation!) he intended to seek powers to sell off the rest of the Common for development as housing. The area to be sold was in two parts; all the land north of the Kingston Road; a large L-shaped slice along the west and south-west of the Common. In other words, most of the land which the Earl intended to sell was in Putney.

The Lord of the Manor made out a good case at the meeting. He explained that the upkeep of the Common cost him a lot of money. It required constant draining. It had to be policed to scare off gypsies and vagrants and to prevent people dumping rubbish on it. The creation of an enclosed Park would prevent such nuisances and would be to the general advantage. Everyone left the meeting very impressed and The Times devoted a leading article to praising the scheme.

But when people got home their enthusiasm abated for it seemed that what they were being offered was the use of 700 acres whereas they had for generations had the use of 1,000 acres. And, they decided, they did not want a formal Park; they wanted what they had – an open Common. They even went so far as to offer to find, by subscription, the money needed for the upkeep of the Common. A committee reported these views to the Earl, but he had made up his mind and the bill had its first reading in Parliament in 1865.

However this Bill was not an isolated event. The growth of London at this time was dramatic and the cause of alarm. Many of its inhabitants were living in grossly overcrowded conditions. The metropolis seemed in imminent danger of suffocation. Accordingly the House of Commons set up a Select Committee to enquire into the preservation of open land in and near the burgeoning city. Lord Spencer's Bill was referred to this Select Committee.

The Earl's legal battle before this Committee was based on the Statute of Merton dating from 1235. This statute was passed when the greater part of England consisted of uncultivable forest and swamp and the enactment was designed to bring this land into production by allowing manorial lords the freedom to enclose common lands provided that enough pasture was left to provide for the needs of villagers. But, said the Earl, centuries of change in manorial custom had extinguished all common rights over the land, leaving him as absolute owner of the Commons.

The Select Committee did not uphold this view however, and reported that it was not expedient that the Commons should be enclosed or that any part of the Common should be sold. In the face of this decision, Lord Spencer first amended his Bill and then (11 May 1865) withdrew it. And that, one might have thought, was the end of the matter.

But a little over two years later we read this description of the Commons:

> Manure-heaps, rubbish, stones, dead animals, and garbage, are crammed together at the corner leading from the village (Wimbledon) to the rifle-butts, making that part of it an eye-sore and a nuisance; turf has been peeled off it almost by the acre; the gorse and heather, of which we were so proud, is being rapidly sacrificed; huge yawning chasms are dug across its principal road, and in the centre of a picturesque dell, which was, until a few months ago, one of its chief beauties, is a huge brick field several acres in extent – in short the

common is being rapidly reduced to the condition attributed to it by the detractors advocating its enclosure, and, unless steps be speedily taken for its protection, London will soon lose a magnificent natural park which no expenditure of public money could replace. In the midst of the piles of rubbish and the manure heaps are boards, saying that it is only by permission of the lord of the manor that anything is deposited there; the workmen engaged in making the road impassable tell you they are improving it, "makin' it more leveller"; those engaged in the brick field say that the clay they dig is destined for drain pipes and bricks to free the common from damp, and to build the lord of the manor a house. Thus, every injury is plausibly spoken of as a public benefit...[1]

The reason for this sordid state of affairs is two-fold. Firstly, the Earl was busy concocting *evidence* that the Commons were in a highly neglected state and that this neglect could only be remedied by the measures which he had proposed in his Bill. And secondly, he was intending to assert by his actions his absolute ownership of the Common. The Lord of the Manor had fiery red hair and a vast spade beard. He was a determined man. He had withdrawn his Bill, but he had not admitted defeat. Indeed he was doing more than was mentioned in the quotation above. Under the assumed name of Hayward he bought up the dairy businesses round the common, so that now no-one, except the Lord of the Manor, was pasturing cattle under the ancient commonage rights. Then he enclosed ten acres on which he pastured sheep. This was intended to prove that he had, if he was not challenged, the right to enclose parts of the Common.

On 1 December 1866 was filed a Bill of Complaint in the Court of Chancery. The case is known as Peek v Earl Spencer. Henry William Peek was the chairman of the Wimbledon Common Defence Committee which had been formed earlier in that year. Lord Spencer took nearly two years to prepare his defence.

Eventually it was agreed that the case should be dropped and a new Bill should be introduced into Parliament. This was done and the Act became law in 1871.

The Act invested control of the Common in eight Conservators while the Lords of the Manor were to receive a perpetual annuity of £1,200 (this was redeemed in 1968). Money for maintenance expenses is raised by means of a Common Rate imposed on every tenant or occupier of a dwelling anywhere in Putney or within three-quarters of a mile of any part of the Common. Three of the Conservators are appointed by the Government. The other five are elected by the people living within the Commons Rate area. The elections are held every three years.

Common lands and other open spaces are always in danger of being gobbled up for some enterprise which is described by their promoters as being to the public benefit. Eight acres of Putney Heath were covered by the reservoirs of the Chelsea Waterworks Company in 1856[2]. In our own times a large area of the Heath was destroyed when the A3 road was extended and the new roundabout was built at Tibbet's Corner.

The financing of the Commons was fundamentally changed by the Government's introduction in 1990 of the Community Charge: Mrs Thatcher's 'Poll Tax'. This abolished domestic rates and the Commons Rate. The Conservators' role as a Rating Authority came to an end and, instead, the Commons were to be financed by means of a Commons Levy, set by the Conservators and collected by the three boroughs in whose area the Commons lie: Kingston, Merton and Wandsworth. Initially this was related to the to the number of people living within the boundaries of the old Commons Rate area and the individual's contribution was to be added on to the Community Charge paid by local residents; after 1993, with the abolition of the Community Charge, it was added to the Council Tax, and this is still the system.

While no doubt it made practical sense for councils rather than the conservators to send out an additional set of rate bills for comparatively small sums, the change had some unexpected repercussions. For instance, Wandsworth Council's decision in 1991, and again in 1992, not to make a Community Charge, meant that Putney and Roehampton residents did not have to pay the Commons Levy – unlike residents in Kingston and Wimbledon! Most recently, in 2009, Wandsworth Council froze its Council Tax, but Putney and Roehampton residents in the Commons rate area had to pay a slightly increased Council Tax due to the rise in the Commons Levy.

Wandsworth council, irritated by such events, made in clear in the 1990's that it wanted to take over the running of Putney Heath and Putney Lower Common. A team from Putney Conservatives stood in the Commons Conservators' election to try to take control – but they were not elected. A group standing as 'Independents' (mainly the existing elected Conservators, were re-elected. The Conservators' elections have always, subsequently, been non-political. Leading figures in the Putney Society have always played a strong role in the Commons Conservators: in the 2009 election, of the five Conservators elected, four were Putney Society members.

Why has the 1871 Wimbledon and Putney Commons Act proved so resilient and survived so long, whilst elsewhere other commons, which had similar legislation, have long since passed into local authority control, Wandsworth Common and Hampstead Heath, for example? The fact that the Commons lie partly in three different London Boroughs and that these boroughs seem to find it difficult to arrive at a shared view on the future of the management of the Commons, as well as the clear dedication of those elected to serve as Commons Conservators, appears to have ensured that the Commons remain securely in the control of local residents - determined to put the interests of the Commons first.

CHAPTER ELEVEN
Literature and Leisure

Putney is associated with many literary figures. Samuel Pepys commented in his diary on 28 April, 1667:

> After dinner by water, the day being mighty pleasant and the tide serving finely… As high as Barne Elmes; and there took one turn alone and then back to Putny Church, where I saw the girls of the school, few of which pretty; and there I came into a pew and met with little James Pierce; which I was much pleased at, the little rogue being very pleased, to see me – his master, Reader to the church. Here was a good sermon and much company, but I sleepy and a little out of order for my hat falling down through a hole underneath the pulpit; which however after sermon, by a stick and the help of the clerk, I got up again.

Edward Gibbon, (1737-1794) who wrote *Decline and Fall of the Roman Empire*, lived in Lime Grove. Residents in the area would be asked by witty friends when answering their telephones whether they were through to "Decline and Fall". James Macpherson, the translator of the Ossianic poems, lived on Putney Heath. Further down, on the High Street, at a house called Chatfield, Leigh Hunt died while on a visit to a friend. Mary Wollstonecraft, author of *The Vindication of the Rights of Women*, lived for a time in Putney and tried to drown herself off Putney Bridge when she was deserted by Captain Imlay.

Sir George Newnes, editor of Tit Bits and founder of the publishing house of Newnes, lived at Wildcroft (on the site of the *Fireproof House*). He was a great friend to Putney since he bought the land and paid for the cost of building Putney's public library. The library, in Disraeli Road, still bears the name. It was opened in 1899.

The most famous of Putney's Victorian literati was Swinburne the poet, (1837-1909) who lived for thirty-odd years with Watts Dunton in a Victorian house at 11 Putney Hill called *The Pines*, which has an

English Heritage blue plaque. Max Beerbohm has given us a superb portrait of Swinburne's last years at Putney and William Gaunt, in *The Aesthetic Adventure*, has shown us how the poet came to Putney and how he fared there. Both books are easily available: but not generally available are these records of Swinburne by those who saw him from a respectable, if slightly humorous, distance:

> A familiar figure walking along the Common from Putney was Swinburne the poet. In his tight little black suit and round black felt hat, with his flaming red hair and beard and bright blue eyes he was seen walking very quickly and springingly from Putney where he lived with Watts Dunton, to take light refreshment at the Rose and Crown (Wimbledon High Street) and perhaps to visit Miss Frost, the stationer, to look at her books and collect one or two. Before he left the shop Miss Frost always 'balanced his pockets', because he would cram several purchases into one pocket and have the other empty; they were great friends, Miss Frost always getting him into her back parlour if many people came into the shop for he was so very shy[1].

and

> At the bottom of Putney Hill there always stood a trace horse to help the green horse bus up the hill. Children used to put pennies in the box to pay for its maintenance. The box was outside The Pines. Sometimes Mr Swinburne would come out and pat the head of a child in a wickermail cart (pram). Sometimes he wore a round white hat.

Margaret Butler (WHS newsletter 15, January 1977)

A famous resident of Putney was Dora, David Copperfield's first bride. Copperfield has this to say of his wedding (which presumably took place in St Mary's Church):

> The rest is all a more or less incoherent dream. A dream of… the clergyman and clerk appearing; of a few boatmen and some other people strolling in; of an ancient mariner behind me, strongly flavouring the church with rum…

This sailor may, in part, explain a mystery. In A Dictionary of English

Phrases by A M Hyamson[2] we find the following unflattering entry:

> Putney, Go to: an expression of impatience. Putney was formerly considered outside the pale of society.

Although this was supposed to be a popular expression (similar ones are reported by the Rev Blomfield Jackson[3]) I have been able to find only one such derogatory reference to the place. This is in The Times of 25 May 1882 in which the art critic says:

> Mr Duncan has evidently conceived Circe as of a rather coarse type of beauty, something like a Putney barmaid[4].

Arnold Bennett, (1867-1931) was a constant visitor and sometime resident of Putney. He set his 1908 intriguing novel *Buried Alive* in Putney with the protagonist Priam Farll living at 29 Werter Road. He had many friends in the area including the pianist Herbert Sharpe who lived at 29 Oxford Road. In the novel Bennett talks of Putney High Street where all was luxury. There was:

> not a necessary in the street. Even the bakers' shops were a mass of sultana and Berlin pancakes – no one slept there now because of the noise of motors

The noble arches of Putney Bridge "divided a first story (sic) of vans and omnibuses from a ground-floor of barges and racing eights." Bennett mentions the "milk-white" buses crossing the bridge to London,[5] the "red causeway" of the railway bridge a few yards further downstream[6] and, in the distance, Priam Farll "could descry the twin towers of the Crystal Palace, more marvellous than mosques." How clearly the novelist captures the essence of Edwardian London when he writes about the massive advertising posters along the Upper Richmond Road:

> There were York hams eight feet high, that a regiment could not have eaten in a month; shaggy and ferocious oxen peeping out of monstrous teacups in their anxiety to be consumed, (and) spouting bottles of ale whose froth alone would have floated the mail steamers pictured on the adjoining sheet.

Putney 1899 – *From Wandsworth & Putney Gas Co's Distribution Map clearly shows Putney Athletic Ground (the site of the Velodrome). Note the increased residential building in the lower part of Putney.*

His description of Oxford Road is superb, with "white-capped girls cleaning door-knobs or windows, or running along the streets, like escaped nuns…. (T)he tradesmen's boys were continually leaping in and out of carts, or off and on tricycles, busily distributing food and drink as though Putney had been a beleaguered city."[7]

J R Ackerley (1896-1967) lived at Star and Garter Mansions where he wrote a number of books charting life in Putney including *My Dog Tulip*. Editor of The Listener, he fostered the careers of a number of major writers, and wrote openly about homosexuality. Amongst his friends were Siegfried Sassoon and E.M Forster (1879-1970), who is depicted with his mother c.1902 at 22 Werter Road. Forster was also friends with writer and founder of the Hogarth Press, Leonard Woolf (1880-1969) who lived at 9 Colinette Road from the age of 11 until he went to Cambridge. He taught Forster to ride on Putney Common.

Laurie Lee (1914-1997) describes finding "a snug little room over an eating-house" in The Upper Richmond Road in his autobiography *As I Walked Out One Midsummer Morning*. Lee who was 19 in 1934 found work as a labourer in Putney and enjoyed the comforts of "Bubble, Squeak, Liver and B, Toad-in-the-Hole, Meat Pudding or Pie" at the café'. In was in this room which "overhung the railway and rocked all day to the passing trains" that Lee first started writing and won a prize for a poem he'd "dashed off with a sixpenny postal order."

Notable poet Gavin Ewart (1916-1995) FRSL who regularly wrote about life in Putney, lived at Kenilworth Court and was commemorated by the Society with a blue plaque in 2009. Another adjacent plaque was placed by the Society in 2009 to Baron Jenkins of Putney, (1908-2004) Minister for the Arts and Putney MP 1964-1979. The first blue plaque placed by the Society in 2007 was at 307 Upper Richmond Road for Antarctic explorer Captain Lawrence Oates (1880-1912). In 2009 the Society also placed at plaque at 32 Landford Road to commemorate photographer Norman Parkinson CBE (1913-1990). In the same year Wandsworth Borough Council launched their green plaque scheme commemorating Clement Richard Attlee, 1st Earl Attlee (1883-1967) Prime Minister 1945-1951 who was born in Putney and lived in Portinscale Road.

Sir William Lancaster, Mayor of Wandsworth in 1902 was an

outstanding benefactor to Putney and Wandsworth. For many years a churchwarden at St Mary's where the Lancaster family donated a set of commemorative doors in 1931, he built a church hall in Putney Bridge Road and endowed Tooting Library. He was the driving force in the creation of the Putney School of Art which moved to its current site in 1906 on land leased from Lancaster at a peppercorn rent. The LCC acquired the freehold in 1924. Lancaster who died in 1929 was associated with the art school for over 40 years. Lancaster is also to be commemorated with a blue plaque at the Art School by the Society.

His grandson Osbert Lancaster was a frequent visitor to Putney before the First World War when he was a small boy. His recollections of these visits provide an amusing glimpse of Edwardian Putney:

> ...my regular expeditions to visit my grandfather on Putney Hill were always enjoyable... they involved a ride on a bus... on the understanding that I was to get out at Putney Station and walk up the Hill. At that date my chief complaint against Putney Hill was the total absence of shops... its immense residential dullness was only occasionally relieved by a steam omnibus bursting into flames on approaching the summit...

His grandfather's home, South Lynn

> ...was a large four-square Victorian mansion in yellow brick set well back from the road behind a semi-circular drive... In the centre of the facade was an imposing front door approached by a flight of white marble steps...

Behind the house

> From the upper garden we descended by a flight of Italianate balustraded steps flanked with geraniums in urns to a region of flower and vegetable beds... and passed admiringly but swiftly to the greenhouses... Beyond the greenhouses lay a coach-house and a yard... and here, were it not for 'The Field', the garden would have ended. 'The Field', which was separated from the main garden by a still surprisingly rural lane, was, curiously enough, all that its name implied... It fulfilled many of the functions of a proper country field, bearing an annual crop of hay and from time to time witnessing church

fetes and school sports, and its apparent size cannot have been wholly illusory as it is today covered by a housing estate[8].

In the 1890s there were nearly 250 cycling clubs in Britain. Putney was a leader in the field and in 1891-1905 had its own cycling and athletic track The Putney Velodrome, situated in the area where Hotham and Landsford Roads are now. The Velodrome met international standards and was an important centre for sporting and social life in the area. World cycling and walking records were set here and events attended by 5,000 – 10,000 people. The grounds were also used by the community as well and in 1903 St Mary's school in Felsham Road held their annual sports day there. In 1894 The Times recorded a 12 hour race in which one of the riders was Arthur Gerhold, the father of Peter Gerhold who co-founded the Putney Society. Arthur Gerhold covered 190 miles 693 yards in the 12 hours. The Wandsworth Borough News reported that "in spite of this heroic effort he only came eighth". A 1890s advertisement for Elliman's embrocation in a cyling magazine of the period entitled "the New Woman rides towards freedom with the man of her choice" depicts a sturdy woman with full Edwardian knickerbockers glory, riding along with her man.

20th century Putney had some extraordinary aspects of opulence. 18 February 1938 The Borough News reported the opening of Zeeta House – Putney's *luxury restaurant and ballroom* (now Foxton's estate agents on the corner of Upper Richmond Road and Putney High Street) The shop was beautifuly designed in silver and gold with heavily carpeted interiors and stairs and a ballroom with oak dance floor. Even the cloakrooms had air conditioning. Further information about Zeeta is seen in the *WBN* advert 20 October 1944, at the height of the V1 rocket attacks. It includes phrases like:

> Morning coffee and light refreshments served in the Café... Luncheons & afternoon teas now served in our beautiful Tudor Room... Our magnificent ballroom available for wedding receptions...

and, most tellingly ...

> Tea dances suspended until further notice

The Society placed a gilded sundial on Zeeta House to mark the Millennium in 2000 featuring its trademark swan, an oar gnoman and the legend: "time like an ever rolling stream".

Touches of this opulence were also reflected in the abundance of cinemas and theatres in Putney which sprang up in the 20th century. There is much evidence in accounts such as Arnold Bennett's description of Putney in 1908 that the residents attended these venues several times a week in preference to going "up West". The advertising for local shows was pitched at "West End quality at half the price".

The Hippodrome Theatre, in Felsham Road opened in 1906. The interior was decorated in Renaissance style with a lofty panelled dome from which hung an elegant chandelier. Over the proscenium was the Borough arms with a scenecloth showing the foot of old Putney bridge with St Mary's church and the Red and White Lion public houses. The famous comedienne Marie Lloyd appeared singing songs like "One of the ruins that Cromwell knocked about a bit". After some use as a cinema the building closed in 1961 but was later used as the set of Vincent Price's film *Theatre of Blood* in 1972 before it was demolished a year later.

Walking down the High Street from the station, you would have seen The Prince's Cinema at number 113, W H Smiths. This was originally used as Assembly Rooms for concerts and pubic meetings 1901. In 1910 The Mystic Picture Theatre company advertised that it would be showing "absolutely flickerless pictures at last". The venue continued to operate under different names probably because of increased competition from other venues, particularly the Mirror cinema in Putney Bridge Road. Afternoon picture teas proved very popular.

Further down the High Street was The Electric Palace Cinema at number 23, on the corner of Putney Bridge road and the High Street. Opened in 1911, this was one of the first purpose-built cinemas and in 1917 was showing films such as Mary Pickford's *The Pride of the Clan*. The cinema was rebuilt in 1926 with the latest cinema organ and renamed frequently before it was eventually demolished in 1971, and replaced by a new cinema complex. The current Odeon cinema next door at 25 Putney High Street was renamed in 2000 after the building was variously an early multiplex ABC in 1975, and prior to that known as The Regal. The Regal which opened there in 1937 had grand sweeping staircases and Saturday morning cinema.

Just round the corner in 222 Putney Bridge Road was The Mirror Cinema also built in 1911. An advertisement at the time described it:

> every seat velvet covered. The most cosy hall in the district. Adults 6d and 3d. Children 3d and 2d. Change of programme Mondays and Thursdays. Open every evening at 6. Matinees Mondays, Thursdays and Saturdays at 3.

It was demolished at the same time as the Palace and Regal cinemas in 1971/2.

CHAPTER TWELVE

Putney at War 1939-45

Commuters standing on Putney Bridge Station looking south towards the river can see one of the 6000 remaining pill boxes. In all 28000 were built in 1940 as Britain prepared for what then seemed like an imminent invasion. Similar, still standing pill boxes were built on the northern ends of Kew and Barnes railway bridges, part of the last line of defence before inner London.

Putney, like the rest of London, was very much on the front line 1940-45. In 1939 air raid trenches and shelters had been built in many back gardens and in Wandsworth Park and Lower Common. The mounds you can see today next to Beverley Brook on the Common were formed by the dumping of hard core from the numerous cleared bomb sites.

Putney High School was evacuated along with most other London schools in 1939 but allowed back the following year after the non event of the phoney war. By the time PHS came back, it had to relocate in Upper Richmond road as the Metropolitan Police had taken over its Putney Hill premises. Other schools were also evacuated. Putney County School, the local girls grammar school, later Mayfield comprehensive and now Ashcroft College, was moved to Woking along with Wandsworth Boys School. Society member Sheila Monaghan remembers that fateful day on September 1 1939, two days before war was declared, when:

> wearing our winter uniforms, carrying our bundles. Complete with labels, and gas masks in cardboard boxes with a piece of string for a shoulder strap, we were assembled and led out onto West Hill. On arrival in Woking we were taken to a centre where we were given a medical examination, told to wash our hands and feet, in cases where the dye from our black woollen stocking had stained them. Our hair was inspected for nits and we were given a thorough going over. No one had any of the scabies, impetigo or ring worm that were being looked for …Well, we were from Mayfield.

In 1939 one of the biggest fears, mainly because of the experiences of wars in Ethiopa, China and Spain, was gas attack on civilians. For this reason Wandsworth Council took delivery of 330,000 gas masks. Many of these were stored in Ashlone Wharf by Beverley Brook. At one point, early in the War, it was compulsory to wear your mask outside, but eventually through the seeming lack of danger these regulations became relaxed and many gas masks ended up in lost property.

But of course the bombers did come. And the results of the 200 odd hits that Putney took in the war can be seen in the streets today. Throughout the town it is easy to spot a break in a terrace, an odd cul de sac, a different brick, an out of place design obviously of a more recent vintage than the largely Edwardian and Victorian homes which form the bulk of dwellings in most of Putney. Many of these are the result of the war damage.

The first bomb hit Putney on 2 September 1940 hitting Roehampton golf course thereby creating a bunker on the 16th fairway. The last V1 rocket bomb hit Putney in August 1944 landing near the Highlands Heath block on Putney Heath. Geoffrey Haines, a business executive who ran the shops and factories for the London Association for the Blind, a free mason and a member of St Margaret's Church, was also an air raid warden and lived in Larpent Avenue. His wife Olive eventually became mayor of Wandsworth. He wrote a seven volume diary which covers the war years and is housed at the Wandsworth Historical Library. On 8 September 1940 when the first bombs fell on Putney dwellings hitting the nearby lawn tennis club he was told by the police to go away. They obviously didn't relish the interference of those they considered amateurs. When the bombs fell again the next night, one ironically on the police station, Haines reports:

> I was welcomed with open arms… they were ashamed of the way they had treated me the previous day.

By the end of the war, Putney had suffered as many as 200 bomb hits and 16 rocket attacks. Sheila Monaghan remembers the air raid wardens being somewhat officious:

> The slightest chink of light they would be banging on the door, shouting

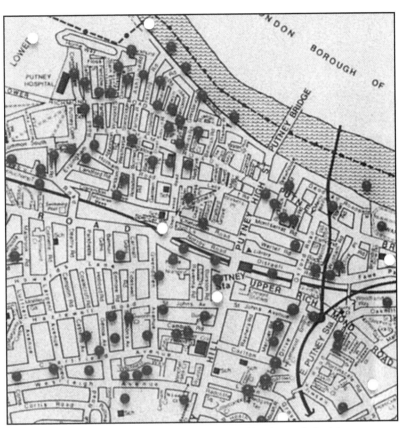

Where the Bombs Fell – *1939-1945 Wandsworth Archives*
Key: (dark dots) High explosive (white dots) V1s (flying bombs)

lights out, thick curtains were not enough. As a school girl I remember
things like exams being disrupted, sharing classes with Wandsworth
School because there was a shortage of teachers and catching the train
down to Woking where the school had been evacuated

Vivienne Hall lived on Putney Hill and worked as a typist in the City. She
kept a dairy of the war years which is housed at the Imperial War
Museum. As Britain's overwhelmed forces retreated towards Dunkirk
she wrote on 25 May l940:

The town(Putney) was very much as usual, people are determinedly cheerful and though one or two announced gloomily that we might as well put our heads in the oven as the Germans would be here any minute most people were still hopeful.

and on 18 September 1940:

Eight at night until six in the morning heaven and earth went mad with noise. The barrage spat into the sky booming and bursting and the planes replied with whining bombs and all manner of horrors. All night the swish and whistle of things falling from the sky kept us on alert- but it passed over. The flashes through the curtains looked like endless lightening and the beastly planes purring overhead made a fantastic accompaniment to the crashing night.

Putney suffered three major hits: the first, during the blitz of August 1940 to May 1941 hit the Castle pub, a relatively modern Young's house at the top of Brewhouse Street which eventually closed early this century. As the Wandsworth Historian wrote:

Even during the *Blitz*, people still went to pubs for a brief escape from the anxieties of the war, and the evening of Saturday 19th April found The Castle in Putney Bridge Road crowded with local people. Late in the evening it was hit by a high explosive bomb, destroying the building, killing 48 and injuring 141.

Christine Sand lived in Cromford Road until 1944 when she joined the WRNS. She was in the fish and chip shop a few doors away from when the Castle pub was hit. She remembers:

me and my friend heard the noise and just made our way down to the shelters in Wandsworth park. At the time you were just grateful it wasn't you, you didn't make a big thing about it, you just got on with it. We had an air raid shelter in our garden and next door had a vegetable patch so we both shared.

Such was the shortage of news print in the War that if you took your own newspaper for wrapping to the fish and chip shop you got a price reduction.

Since there had been very few raids in 1942 and throughout most of 1943, people had become more confident, perhaps even complacent, and took full advantage of what little entertainment was available. This changed dramatically in the evening of Sunday, 7 November 1943 after the third period of air raids had started, when the second major hit occurred, the worst incident of the war in the two boroughs (Battersea and Wandsworth) occurred. An air raid warning was sounded at about 8.40 pm, with few people going to air raid shelters. At 9.02 pm a lone aircraft released a single 500 kg Stabo high explosive bomb that hit No. 35 Putney High Street, which is opposite the end of Felsham Road, causing great damage on the east side of the High Street.

> The worst feature was the extensive casualties in the Black and White Milk Bar on the ground floor of No. 35, and upstairs the 'Cinderella Dance Club', at the time a very popular venue in Putney for young people. In addition to these, a number of people were killed and injured in the High Street, who had been walking or standing at bus stops. A total of 81 were killed, 46 females and 35 males, with 248 injured, many of them seriously, including 18 service personnel killed and 26 injured. The youngest killed was Edward Henry Smith, aged 14, of 196B Fulham Palace Road. This air raid brought great grief to many families and to Putney, since nearly two-thirds of the casualties were young people under 23 years of age.[1]

Tony Pink, who has lived for many years in Erpingham Road, remembers going from the Cricketers pub (now a Wills Art Gallery on the Lower Richmond Road) to see the devastation:

> It was a terrible scene, blood and smoke every where, all those bodies being pulled out but you got used to them.

But although historians may dwell on the major incidents, each bomb which landed had an effect. As Vivienne Hall when the bombs hit Putney Hill wrote on 19 Feb 1944:

> What a night! The hideous well remembered swaying of the house as one after another came the thumps of near bombs – the frightening roar of the plane as it dived to deliver its message and then the crump and tinkle of breaking glass. How I hate myself for being sick with fear,

but there it is, I looked out and saw the red glow of fire all around us. It ended of course and then out to see next door had its drive blown into the road, our garden wall was down, the garage opposite had disappeared, a delayed action bomb was sitting in the road and two old ladies had been killed as they had tried to get to their shelter. Smoke was everywhere, seven houses were on fire in Gwendolen Avenue and there was a huge blaze in Wandsworth. We were lucky a few cracked windows and some bricks scattered about the garden and drive.

After D day on the 7 June 1944, Londoners felt that not only was the end of the War in sight but they had definitely seen the end of the bombing. But of course then came the VI rockets which started on the night of the 13 June when a single VI exploded in Bow. The real assault commenced in the night of 15/16 June, and the first three deaths occurred in Battersea on Saturday, 17 June.

On Sunday, 18 June came one of the worst days for the boroughs of Wandsworth and Battersea when 101 were killed, and 595 injured, almost the highest number of deaths in a single day throughout the war. Putney's third major hit was on this day. At about 9.15am, a V1 damaged by anti-aircraft fire, crashed and exploded at the junction of the Upper Richmond Road and Charlwood Road, Putney, killing 36 and injuring 25.

Geoffrey Haines, the warden on duty, wrote of this incident:

> At every corner of the block of flats people were leaning out, shouting for help, as the rear of the building had been destroyed by blast and a fire had started in the shops beneath.

The blast had been powerful enough to lift the roof of the Methodist church across the road. Over 300 members of the emergency services were involved in putting out the flames, ferrying the dead and wounded, clearing the wreckage and eventually destroying what was left of the building. The office of Air Malta now stands on the site.

This attack happened on the same day that a V1-doodlebug hit the Guards Chapel in St James killing 141. The three weeks from the 18 June saw over 100 rockets a week hit London with nearly 1000 deaths. The last V1 fell on the Town on Putney Heath near the Highland Heath block of flats in August 1944. The last fell on London in March 1945.

And when the rockets starting falling in June 1944 Vivienne Hall wrote:

> I thought the blitzes were frightening but this horrible machine is worse, you are always listening. Always waiting for the drone of the machine getting closer and closer-oh hell it's a hateful business. As I was trying to have a bath on Sunday at 10.15 a burst of gun fire and the drone of the engine meant another was passing over. There was a complete silence, then a terrific explosion and the inevitable wrench of torn wood and bricks and windows tinkling to bits. I forgot about washing my back and threw on my clothes, a most unpleasant feeling clothes on a wet soapy body.

On 7 April l945 Germany surrendered. For six years Putney like the rest of London had put up with a lot more than soapy backs. Because the bombers invariably followed the Thames as path finder, Putney, which could never have been a prime target suffered probably more than its fair share of bomb damage. For many the War ended with a bit of whimper. When peace was declared Geoffrey Haines would write in his best suburban style:

> I was at home at the time… this end of the war was taken quite calmly.

Not so elsewhere as an exhausted people showed their relief with street parties and sometimes wild celebrations especially among young service people who now no longer were facing death. 11000 attended one such party held over two days in the grounds of a local politician's large house on West Hill. The many bomb sites provided ample wood for the bonfires which lit up the sky. On the 12th of May the US airforce did a victory fly past over London. For the first time in five years people cheered rather than rushed to their air raid shelters.

CHAPTER THIRTEEN
Putney and the Seventies

I n November 1959 the Putney Society was formed as a registered charity to support the aims of the Civic Trust. Since then the amenity society for Putney and Roehampton has brought pressure to bear on those responsible for the local environment: planning, transport, community as well as organised talks and social events.

In the 1970s and 80s Judge Ian Fife (Chairman of the Putney Society 1971-1980 who died in 1990) probably worked harder than anyone else to improve the amenities of Putney and Roehampton. Putney Library contains reminders of him, including the Putney Mural which he commissioned from the artists Arthur Watson and Judith Evans, and which the Putney Society presented to the library on permanent loan in 1979.

One of Judge Fife's most successful projects was to persuade the Borough Council, in the early 1970s, not to sell Ashlone Wharf for commercial development but to extend Leaders Gardens (on Putney Embankment) over Ashlone Road and the Wharf to Beverley Brook. The Putney Society supported this scheme with a 3,500 signature petition.

It is worth recording the origins of another major annual event in Putney's calendar; the Putney Show. Again, this was one of Ian Fife's initiatives. He saw the potential of the Queen's Silver Jubilee in 1977 as a way of bringing the local community together in a unique celebration on Putney Lower Common. With the assistance of the Borough Council, this took place on the weekend of 25 and 26 June 1977. The following week The Wandsworth Borough News carried a front-page headline: "Yes, It Was Non-stop Jubilee Fun!" and reported:

> Over 30,000 people flocked to Putney Lower Common over the
> weekend to take part in this year's jubilee celebrations. And – despite
> the generally cool and overcast weather – it turned out to be worth

every minute of their time, as everybody was given the chance to enjoy an unprecedented range of events which had been specially laid on by Wandsworth Borough Council.

The attractions listed included a steam-engine grand parade, steam-engine games, a Gavioli fair organ, a story-telling Womble, Punch and Judy, clowns, horse show events, wellie-throwing, Derico Alizana's High Wire Act and displays by the Wimbledon Pony Club, the Royal Academy of Dancing, the 4th Putney Scout Group, Morris dancers, a Polish dance group, an escapologist, a medieval music group and Theatre Street players.

The report continues:

There was ice-cream and candy-floss in abundance, and a number of local organisations had set up stalls – including Wandsworth Historical Society, Putney Round Table, Putney Common Association, Wandsworth IVS, Putney Society, 1st Roehampton Venture Scout Unit (climbing section), Roehampton Garden Society and Wimbledon Pony Club... and everyone showed by their enthusiasm what a non-stop success it was.

And so the Putney Show was born, but sadly only lasted until 1992 when Wandsworth Borough Council announced it could no longer provide funding for the annual show

One of the most significant civic battles of the 1970s was the demise under a tidal wave of opposition of much feared *Ringway 2* which would have followed the railway line and essentially led to a motorway driven through the heart of the town. The idea had been to revamp the North and South circular roads with motorways. This particular one would have gone from Chiswick to Clapham Junction across Barnes Common and through Putney .

As Chris Marshall of CBRD states," The plan was simply to draw a line and bulldoze every building that stood in its way." In fact such was the opposition to this scheme which was sponsored by the ruling Conservative party at the Greater London Council at County Hall (the predecessor to the GLA) that they were voted out and Labour under the colourful Ken Livingstone took power.

Looking back one can see that these and other schemes which never saw the light of day were all part of the understandable trend in the 1960s, after the War and the austere 1950s, to update Britain and modernise its infrastructure-regardless of cost.

As chairman of the Putney Society Judge Ian Fife wrote "Many of the schemes for redevelopment ended up in the planners' waste paper baskets. Shortage of public money and the death of the property boom of the early 1970s have a lot to do with this,"

Equally, however, it has been the outcome of a great deal of time and energy spent by local people, arguing at public meetings and inquiries the case for the conservation of the best features of the environment and for the quiet and safety of the inhabitants.

This popular desire to keep things as they are accounts for the mushrooming of Conservation Areas across Putney and Roehampton. Empowered by the Civic Amenities Act of 1967, and informed by studies prepared by the Putney Society, the Borough Council first designated conservation areas covering Charlwood Road, Lifford Street, Coalecroft Road and Parkfields, Putney Embankment, Putney Lower Common, Roehampton Village and the Nelson Houses on the Upper Richmond Road. These were followed later by much larger designations embracing Deodar Road, Dover House Estate, East Putney, Landford Road, Oxford Road, Putney Heath, Rushholme Road, Victoria Drive, Westmead and West Putney, and in March 2001 the major part of the Alton Estate was included as a conservation area.

Together with the eighty or so buildings in Putney and Roehampton individually listed by the Department of the Environment as being of "special architectural or historic interest", and therefore covered by legislation intended to secure their preservation, some one-third of the entire area is now protected from unsympathetic development and change.

CHAPTER FOURTEEN
Bestride The Millennium

B y the end of the l970s there were reasons to be pessimistic about the future of Putney. A spread of anonymous office and apartment blocks and the sprawl of the High Street led many to feel that Putney as a town was losing its way. However fears that the town would degenerate into a dull dormitory suburb were not well founded. In the 1980s instead Putney became something of a boom town – almost a destination leisure centre, a thriving inner city suburb with good shopping ,a range of service industries and extremely healthy amenities. Not least the period has seen the Putney Society grow to over 1000 members with an active involvement in many areas of local life.

Schools and churches have flourished, as a growing number of professional families moved in and demanded more of their local services. Typical of environmental, cultural, social and transport trends – while in 1980 there was only one very specialist bike shop in Putney – by 2009 there were four dedicated to serving a wide public. In that period there was also a similar growth in the number of art galleries. Both signs of Putney being at the positive end of national trends. In these cases to do with health and wealth.

In the period 1980-2008 house prices in Putney went up between 10 and 20 times. A semi detached bought at the beginning of the period for £70,000 was sold at the end for £1.25m. The explosion in the Putney property market was illustrated by the number of estate agent firms in the town growing from around six in the mid 1970s to as many as 25 in 2009.

A leading Putney agent throughout the post 1980 period, Tim Warren, said:

> The boom started with people moving from Fulham to bigger houses with gardens from a more expensive and less green Fulham. They

were attracted by the growing number of nursery and prep schools. Most of which have sprung up in that period. The large numbers of modern and converted flats in Putney are a major reason supporting its growth as a leisure centre. Good transport facilities made it popular with City workers who just want a convenient lock up and go address.

As an indication of the increased wealth and property activity, Wandsworth Council reported that between 1980-2008 the number of planning applications went from 1000 a year to over 5000. They ranged in scale from loft conversions to major developments. Putney's contribution to this increase is similar to the rest of the borough.

Typically, at the beginning of the 1980s many Putney streets would be without one conservatory. By the end of the period few houses would be without one. While the 80s were the decade of the conservatory, the 90s were the decade of the loft conversion and the new century saw many home owners digging deep to develop their basements and cellars. At the same time many were turning their front gardens into parking lots as the council brought in parking restrictions as a way of keeping commuters from parking in local streets.

A side effect of London becoming a leading world finance centre was the influx of foreign nationals to the City and its high salaries. The number of large flats in Putney plus its proximity and good transport links to this financial centre attracted Japanese, Europeans, Russians not to mention Australians and South Africans. All of whom not only supported the property market, specialist shops but also the growing number of preparatory, nursery and day care places which grew up in the town over the period.

Putney's desirability as a green riverside suburb within cycling distance of the West End, and also well served by public transport, has made it the subject of every property trend going.

In the l960s there was a desperate shortage of office space. East Putney, along the Upper Richmond Road became the home for several office blocks. As the housing boom took over, so developers looked to converting these work stations into blocks of flats. The most successful was the conversion of the old ICL building by St Mary's church.

Its superb riverside location became Putney Wharf Tower, one of the most prestigious riverside luxury blocks in London. Similar residential developments can be seen along the Thames from Richmond to Canary Wharf and for that matter on every river bank in every major city throughout the first world.

As part of these Thameside developments, a river bus service was established in 2006. Three boats go east in the morning, and return from the City in the evening. This had been unsuccessful in the 1990s, but the service run by Thames Executive Charters was far more professional. Also it had local government approval, if not financial support. The result being it had every chance of being a permanent feature.

Until the 1980s Putney was also home to various light industries from the production of dog guards in Dryburgh Road, tennis balls and window blinds in Deodar Road to the Calor Gas and Shell depots by Wandsworth Park.

The milk depot in Lower Richmond Road and the laundry in Putney Bridge Road became smart new residential developments. The milk depot itself was left over from the 19th century Morrison's dairy and farm which operated on Lower Common until the 1880s. While some of these premises have been converted into offices space, more have become desirable apartment dwellings, along the river.

The history of ICL, since it is linked to Putney is worth retelling. The ICL building was originally designed by Richard Siefert, architect of Jubilee House and Centrepoint.

Sponsored by central government, International Computers Limited was the UK's answer to IBM. It had office blocks on both sides of Putney Bridge. It was founded in 1968, and eventually closed its doors in 2002. It had previously quit Putney, having been taken over by the Japanese firm Fujitsu. For a while fuelled by government contracts, it prospered, but increasingly the company wilted under foreign competition and the switch from main frame to personal computers. Today the buildings which once represented a major part of the UK's computer industry have transformed themselves – becoming an expensive apartment block south of the river and a budget price out of town hotel on the north side. Both buildings are eminently successful in their present roles, but both are metaphors for the decline and fall of the UK's industrial base.

The trend for eating out, increased leisure and the disposable wealth of young people saw Putney get upgraded, and often gastro, pubs, more and better restaurants and a whole range of coffee bars. As late as 1980 Putney only had half a dozen restaurants. Today there are over thirty though typically they serve the lower to mid range rather than those seeking haute cuisine.

Putney may have become prosperous but it has not become and may never be overly fashionable. Typically, the architects' iconic Putney Bridge Restaurant was originally conceived as an expensive haute cuisine restaurant but failed as that and was taken over by a main stream Thai eaterie. The restaurant built in 1995 took the place of a garage which had its moment of fame, as it was on its premises that the serial murderer John Christie was arrested in 1953.

When one considers the sad fate of farmers markets and up market patisseries – especially in relation to their success in nearby Barnes one should remember that Putney is now well catered for by the very best and varied of food supermarkets.

However although family houses may have grabbed the Putney headlines during the 1980-2009 period, flat dwellers are the majority. There are six social housing estates in and around Putney, and many large houses have been converted into three and five apartment dwellings. There are also the considerable private blocks in East Putney, on the Upper Richmond Road and up Putney Hill. Retailers in Putney have long been aware that singles and couples renting have represented a sizeable share of the market

The financial group Merrill Lynch's study in 2004 of Putney *Retail Strategy for the Exchange Shopping Centre* showed that 55% of the local population were what they called *Urban Intelligent*, that is well educated young singles attracted to Putney by its good connections with the centre and suitable accommodation. The national percentage for this group is eight. 22% of Putney dwellers are *Symbols of Success* – i.e. successful middle aged families. That is more than double the national average for this group. But significantly 11.5% are classed as *Welfare Borderline* (national average 7%). This last group are younger, lower income, large and single parent families.

For many the boat houses and what they represent are the symbol of Putney. At the beginning of the period some boat houses were sold off as offices and many feared that that could become a trend. In fact Putney Rowing Club moved out of its "boat house" in the basement of The Dukes Head and went to Chiswick Bridge. However the thirty years since 1980 saw real growth in British rowing, highlighted by increasingly dramatic Olympic success.

Since the 1970s there has also been a massive growth in women's rowing. Thames RC admitted women in 1973 and the London Rowing Club followed some time later in 2002. All the major clubs have since upgraded their facilities so as to be able to cater for the highly technical training schedules of modern athletes. All this has led to the clubs enjoying increased membership. As well in the new century major private schools – Dulwich College, Kings Wimbledon and Westminster established their Boat Houses on the Embankment.

Every year Putney and the river achieve national media coverage when the Oxford and Cambridge Boat Race takes place. Crowds gather on Putney Embankment to watch the start of the race, which is marked by a stone – inscribed UBR – beside Putney Pier. Those who live locally hurry home to watch the finish on television. It is an event to be experienced!

Similarly, the river comes to life when the Head of the River Race is held each March. Established in the late 1920s, nowadays it involves 400 crews rowing in a processional race on a timed basis from Mortlake to Putney. The Putney Town Regatta, which dates from 1911, is still an annual May time attraction.

The 80s saw the reconstruction of the Embankment's river wall with smart new railings, lamps and paving stones, though some were sorry to see the old, more open railings go. An addition to the attraction of the Embankment was Alan Thornhill's bronze sculpture *Load*, presented to Putney by the sculptor in April 1989. Alan presented another seven sculptures to the borough which now form a sculpture trail from Wandsworth Park to Leader's Gardens.

St Mary's church by the bridge, recovered from its devastating fire in 1973 and financed its highly successful rebuild by selling St John's to the Polish Catholic church. However the Church of England in Putney suffered, along with the rest of the country something of a congregation loss in the 1960-80 period. In fact in 2000 the large United Reform Church faced with rising costs and declining congregations on the Upper Richmond Road was bulldozed to make way for yet more apartments.

After an arson attack in 1993, All Saints, famous for its Burne Jones/William Morris windows, received over £1m in refurbishment grants from English Heritage and local donations.

The decline in C of E attendance fell so much that plans were a foot in the 1980s to sell off All Saints on Lower Common. However the appointment of Jonathan Draper as vicar in 1991 reversed this state of affairs. By 2000 both All Saints and St Mary's were bucking the national trend and had become thriving parishes. When Draper was promoted to York Minster this rude health continued under the high profile stewardship of Giles Fraser whose media appearances and Chelsea football shirt made him one of the best known vicars in Britain. Giles' inspiration and winning of a Guardian newspaper prize not only established a permanent exhibition celebrating the Putney Debates of 1647, but created the momentum for the highly successful events which celebrated the Debates in 2007.

There has also been the great leap forward in the standard of Putney's schools, especially those at primary level. In 1980 only All Saints rated a mention, but by 2000 All Saints, without slipping, had been overtaken in its academic scores by other local schools. Not least was Our Lady of Victories, which at the beginning of the period lagged a long way behind, but topped the table in 2000.

Cynics would say that the excellence of these largely church primary schools has helped swell the congregations. There is some anecdotal evidence that this is true. Churches have noted some stop attending after their child has got a place at the church school. It is worthwhile noting that Elliot School during this period moved from being a school of second or third choice to one which achieves a regular stream of Oxbridge places.

The much lamented, one time nationally rated, Wandsworth School after a twenty year gap had its site at last replaced by a C of E secondary school. Putney did well out of successive government's commitment to an increased educational spending plan.

Politically "The right to buy" policy introduced by Margaret Thatcher in the l980s crucially changed the social profile of the large Roehampton estates. This and the increased wealth in the Town shifted Putney slowly but inexorably to the right of radical Labour MP Hugh Jenkins, first elected in 1964. He was succeeded by Tory David Mellor in 1979. When Jenkins went to the Lords in l981 he took the title Baron Jenkins of Putney. He died in 2004.

Mellor represented Putney with some gusto until l997 and he always remained popular, and at one Putney Society dinner the chair introduced him by saying, "Nancy always says the naughty boys are the nicest".

At three succeeding elections he succeeded in beating national trends and even when he lost his seat it was in the most extraordinary circumstances. Larger than life financier Sir James Goldsmith led and bank rolled the anti EU Referendum Party. Goldsmith chose to stand in Putney. Many others (ten in all) including the Gun Lobby, Natural Law and the Pro Hunt groups put up candidates and when the result was announced Mellor bitterly attacked Goldsmith and his "derisory 3.5% vote". On live television Goldsmith then responded with the chant of "Out,Out,Out" aimed at Mellor.

Mellor was succeeded by Labour's Tony Colman a one time Burton (now Arcadia, Top Shop etc) fashion group director and head of Merton Council who held Putney for Labour until 2005 when a slight Tory swing led to Putney being one of the few seats that moved to the right.

Justine Greening, has proved an energetic local MP in the lead fighting against Heathrow expansion, a cause which all Putney MPs have to espouse. One of the defences the pro airport lobby uses is the fact that aircraft noise has had no effect on Putney house prices. Greening, like Jenkins and Mellor soon became a very visible opposition spokesman.

At Town Hall level, a left wing Labour Council was ousted in the late 1970s by a right wing Tory Council, which was one of the first to espouse privatised services, and which has consistently if sometimes controversially, kept Council tax low while at the same time maintaining reasonable levels of services. The selling of the land of the Putney garden centre, the closure of the Wandsworth Museum and the demise of the Robert Joy Day Centre, although in neighbourhood terms very unpopular, did little to dent this Tory flagship's electoral popularity in Putney and the rest of Wandsworth.

In fact even the one time Labour heartland of Roehampton was by 2007 returning Tory councillors, not least because of the change of ownership on the estates. Despite massive Labour swings nationally during the 1990s, the local Tories claim of being the "best value for money" council has kept them in control of Wandsworth Town Hall.

The most significant change in Putney town centre in 1990 was the development of the old Ferry Works site on the west side of the High Street. Here Guardian Royal Exchange created Putney Exchange shopping centre. The architects, Chapman Taylor and Partners, produced a fine scheme of shop units in a light and airy enclosed mall, with rooftop car park and some flats above the new Lacy Road shops: all in a style blending well with existing buildings. It was unfortunate that the opening in 1990 coincided with an economic recession which blighted the retail market – but the quality of the scheme should assure its long term success, despite the counter attraction of out of town shopping developments such as the Asda Superstore which replaced the old Smiths' Industries building in Roehampton Vale in 1989.

There is also a Tale of two Hospitals. Queen Mary's Roehampton was between 2003-6 gradually knocked down and then rebuilt to fit in with the grander Primary Health Trust plan involving St Georges Tooting and

Kingston. The surplus land was typically dedicated to a large housing development. From start to finish a three year project which despite local reservations about the loss of an Accident and Emergency Unit went very smoothly. Many point to the efficiency springing from this project being funded by a £55m Private Funding Initiative rather than central or health service funds.

The same Wandsworth Primary Health Trust, ten years after the closure of Putney Hospital on the Common, still had not started to either demolish the old building or start to build the health centre, containing the GP's surgeries plus private dwellings that had long been promised. Various pressure groups not least the Putney Society challenged the delay. It has been estimated that the hospital in its disused state was costing the local Health Service in the region of £1m a year, through lost grants, security costs etc.

Since the 1980s in Roehampton, resulting from the selling off of the Alton estate – there are private landlords who now own as many as 100 flats. This was mirrored at the turn of the century by the establishment and growth of Roehampton University. The University, officially opened in 2004 is now 8000 strong with 1,500 staff. It is the result of bringing together on one modern campus the teacher training colleges of on site Digby Stuart and Froebel, with the newly introduced Whitelands and Southland Colleges. As more and more students (and home owners) live on the Alton Estate there have been tensions between the original low income families. Parts of Roehampton have become the most isolated areas in Wandsworth.

Ex mayor of Wandsworth, long time Putney councillor and one time Inspector of the local police Jim Maddan said:

> The establishment of the Night Economy had been a deliberate policy by the Council. It not only brought life and business to parts of the High Street and elsewhere which were dead but it recognised that there was shopping done round the clock not just nine to five. Putney is busier at 10 in the evening than it is at 10 in the morning.

Part of the Brewhouse Street development included the community centre built onto St Mary's, the Brewer Building. This has greatly contributed to social, community and active life in Putney as a whole range of groups use its upgraded meeting rooms, situated in the middle of the Town with the added facility of very good snack bar.

Putney will always attract developers and there will always be vested and selfless interests who will question and oppose both the best and worst intentioned development proposals. It is part of the democratic process of which the Putney Society is proud to be part.

And how much say does the local community have? An organised community can have a real influence in guiding the decision makers in local and central government and this is why groups like the Putney Society, the amenity society for Putney and Roehampton, can play a significant role in shaping our local history. Having read this book, perhaps you ought to become a member so you can play your part too! Ask for details in Putney Library, Disraeli Road, or consult the website **www.putneysociety.org.uk**

REFERENCES AND NOTES ON THE TEXT

1. Beginnings

[1] Much of the archaeological evidence is from Wandsworth Historical Society excavations. Many old river finds are in the collections of the British Museum and the Museum of London, though there are others collections around the country, even abroad.

Palaeolithic finds are extensively cited in the works of John Wymer.

Dates quoted as 'cal BC' are calibrated radiocarbon dates, that is, converted into calendar dates. In effect the Mesolithic to Iron Age dates cited largely owe their dating to radiocarbon, and would have been calibrated at some point.

The following abbreviations are used:

WHS	Wandsworth Historical Society
MoL	Museum of London
BM	British Museum
Colls	Collections

[2] There are several studies of the early environment in this area, some unpublished. Those used here are Rackham and Sidell 2000; Wilkinson *et al* 2000; Branch and Green 2004; Perry and Skelton 1995; notes from Rackham; Jeff Perry pers. com.; Rackham and Scaife, 1997.

[3] Nicholas Lane's map is on display in St Mary's Parish Church, Putney High Street, SW15. A detailed study of the map has been made by Dorian Gerhold (1994).

[4] Extensive discussion, further references and lists of metal finds of the middle and late Bronze Ages are to be found in Rowlands 1976; O'Connor 1980; Needham and Burgess 1980 and particularly in the galleries and collections of the Museum of London and the British Museum.

[5] WHS Excavations, site code BEV I. Dating of this assemblage is based on its similarities to one with radiocarbon dating from Fairfield Park in the Chilterns published by Webley *et al* 2007; both have early examples of rotary querns (hand-mills).

[6] There are a number of these tin-bronze coins from the area but many have vague provenances because some finders have been unwilling to be precise. Local information is available in Cotton and Wood 1996, 22-28, the WHS archive, and Haselgrove 1987, 288; the revised date range for potin coins of late 2nd - early 1st century BC is from Gruel and Haselgrove 2007.

[7] Summarized in the map of Roman Putney and discussed in Farrant 1975; 1977; 1980; 1981;1982; Fuentes 1988;1989a; 1991;1994; Fuentes and Greenwood 1993. Roman burials are frequently found alongside roads or associated with boundaries, hence their use in reconstructing the road system in Putney.

[8] The general character of the settlement and its excavations is described in Farrant 1972, the works by Farrant and Fuentes (formerly Farrant) cited in note 7 and in Fuentes and Greenwood 1993. Some animal bone was initially examined by Marjorie Greenwood and later by Alison Locker, cited in Locker unpublished faunal report, and Armitage *et al* 1987. Charcoals from Bemish Road were identified by Caroline Cartwright, unpublished reports 1975 and 1977. Dr Malcolm Lyne examined some of the pottery groups and has discussed some very late examples; a few are listed in Lyne and Jefferies 1979.

References

Data from WHS excavations and collections, Wandsworth Historical Society Newsletter,

Armitage, P, Locker, A, and Straker, V, 1987 'Environmental Archaeology in London: A Review' in Keeley, H (ed), 1987 *Environmental Archaeology – A Regional Review*, 264ff.

Barrett, J, and Bradley, R (eds), 1980 *Settlement and Society in the British Later Bronze Age* British Archaeol Report 83.

Barron, H Brayson, J, Aldiss, D, Woods, M, and Harrison, A, 2008 *Geodiversity of London* Greater London Authority Consultation Draft July 2008.

Branch, N, and Green, C, 2004 'The environmental history of Surrey' in Cotton *et al* (eds) 2004, 1-18.

British Geological Survey, 1998 *South London solid and drift edition* 1:50 000 Series 270.

Bird, C, 1977 'A Palaeolithic Implement from Putney' *Wandsworth Historian* 17, 12-13.

Bird, D, 2004 *Roman Surrey.*

Bird, J, and Bird, D (eds), 1987 *The Archaeology of Surrey to 1540* Surrey Archaeological Society.

Brudenell, M, 2008 'Reclaiming the Early Iron Age in eastern England' in Davis *et al* 2008, 185-198.

Burnett, A, 1987 *Coin Hoards from Roman Britain Volume VII* British Museum Occasional Paper No 59.

Cartwright, C, 1975 and 1977 Identification of charcoals from Bemish Road sites BEM II and BEM III and Barn Elms, BEV I (unpublished report).

Celoria, F, 1965 'Archaeological Finds from the Counties of London and Middlesex added to the Collections of the London Museum during 1962' *Trans London and Middlesex Archaeol Soc* 21 pt 2, 140-142, plate I.

Clark, J, Cotton, J, Hall, J, Sherris, R, and Swain, H (eds), 2008 *Londinium and Beyond: Essays on Roman London and its hinterland for Harvey Sheldon* CBA Res Rep 156.

Coles, B, 2006 *Beavers in Britain's Past* WARP Occasional Paper 19.

Cotton, J, and Field, D (eds), 2004 *Towards a New Stone Age: Aspects of the Neolithic in South-East England* CBA Res Rep 137

Cotton, J, and Green, A, 2004 'Further Prehistoric Finds from Greater London' *Trans London Middlesex Archaeol Soc* 55, 119-151.

Cotton, J, and Merriman, N, 1991 'Some recent prehistoric finds from Greater London' *Trans London Middlesex Archaeol Soc* 42, 33-57.

Cotton, J, with Johnson, R, 2004 'Two decorated Peterborough bowls from the Thames at Mortlake and their London context' in Cotton and Field (eds) 2004, 128-147.

Cotton, J, and Wood, B, 1996 'Recent prehistoric finds from the Thames Foreshore and beyond in Greater London' Trans London Middlesex Archaeol Soc 47, 1-33.

Cotton, J, Crocker, G, and Graham, A (eds), 2004 *Aspects of Archaeology & History in Surrey: Towards a Research Framework for the County* Surrey Archaeological Society.

Cowan, C, and Hinton, P, 2008 'The Roman Garden in London' in Clark *et al* 2008, 75-81

Cowie, R, and Blackmore, L (eds), 2008 *Early and Middle Saxon rural settlement in the London Region* Museum of London Archaeological Service Monograph 41.

Davis, O, Sharples, N, and Waddington, K (eds), 2008 *Changing perspectives on the first millennium BC.*

Ellaby, R, 2004 'Food for thought: a late Mesolithic site at Charlwood, Surrey' in Cotton and Field (eds) 2004, 12-23.

Farrant, N, 1972 'The Romano-British settlement at Putney' *London Archaeologist* 1.16, 368-71.

Farrant, N, 1975 'The Roman Road System in and around Putney' Wandsworth Historian 13, 1-7.

Farrant, N, 1977 'Excavation at 22 Bendemeer Road, Putney: An Interim Report' *Wandsworth Historian* 17, 11-12.

Farrant, N, 1980 'Felsham Road Excavation – an Interim Report: Part 1 General Background with Prehistoric and Roman Periods' *Wandsworth Historian* 26, 1-10.

Farrant, N , 1981 'Felsham Road Excavation – An Interim Report: Part 2 The Post Roman Periods' *Wandsworth Historian* 29, 1-9.

Farrant, N, 1982 'Felsham Road Archaeological Site – A Further Report' *Wandsworth Historian* 33, 8-14.

Fuentes, N, 1988 'Kingsmere Close Excavation – an interim report: Part 1, the earlier periods' *Wandsworth Historian* 54, 4-8, 26.

Fuentes, N, 1989a 'Crossing Points of the Thames at Putney – Part 1' *Wandsworth Historian* 57, 7-14.

Fuentes, N, 1989b 'Roman Wandsworth: Part 1, Battersea' *Wandsworth Historian* 58,1-8.

Fuentes, N, 1991 'Roman Wandsworth: Part 2. Wandsworth Town' *Wandsworth Historian* 62, 16-26.

Fuentes, N, 1994 'Roman Putney' in Gerhold (ed) 1994a, 11-12.

Fuentes, N, and Greenwood, P, 1993 *Roman Putney* a leaflet published by Wandsworth Historical Society.

Gerhold, D (ed), 1994a *Putney and Roehampton Past.*

Gerhold, D, 1994b *Putney in 1636: Nicholas Lane's Map* Wandsworth Historical Society Occasional Paper 7.

Greenwood, P, 1986a 'Prehistoric Wandsworth: part 1.' *Wandsworth Historian* 48, 1-8

Greenwood, P, 1986b 'Prehistoric Wandsworth: part 2: Postglacial changes in the Mesolithic period' *Wandsworth Historian* 50, 1-8.

Greenwood, P, 1987 'Prehistoric Wandsworth: part 3, the Neolithic Period' *Wandsworth Historian* 52, 15-22.

Greenwood, P, 1988 'Another Tranchet Axe from the Thames' *Wandsworth Historian* 56, 19.

Greenwood, P, 1997 'Iron Age London; some thoughts on *Current Knowledge and Problems* 20 years on' London Archaeologist 8, 153-61.

Greenwood, P, 2008 'Putney (Surrey)' (on the fish trap at Putney) in Cowie and Blackmore (eds) 2008, 116-118.

Greenwood, P, Perring, R, and Rowsome, P, 2006 *From Ice Age to Essex: a history of the people and landscape of East London*. Museum of London Archaeology Service.

Gruel, K, and Haselgrove, C, 2007 'British Potins Abroad: A new find from Central France and the Iron Age in Southeast England' in Gosden, C, Hamerow, H, de Jersey, P and Lock, G (eds) *Communites and Connections: Essays in Honour of Barry Cunliffe* 2007, 240-262.

Hammerson, M, and Hall, J, 1987 'A Hoard from the Thames Foreshore' in Burnett (ed) 1987, 201-204.

Harmon, C, and Quilliec, B (eds), 2008 *Hoards from the Neolithic to Metal Ages* British Archaeol Report International Series 1758.

Lawrence, G, 1929 'Antiquities from the Middle Thames' *Archaeol J* 86, 69-98.

Haselgrove, C, 1987 *Iron Age coinage in Southeast England: the archaeological context* British Archaeol Rep 174.

Haselgrove, C, and Pope, R (eds), 2008 *The Earlier Iron Age in Britain and the near Continent*.

Lewis, J, 2000a 'The Lower Palaeolithic Period' in Museum of London Archaeology Service 2000, 29-43.

Lewis, J, 2000b 'The Upper Palaeolithic and Mesolithic Periods' in Museum of London Archaeology Service 2000, 45-62.

Lowther, A, 1945 'Caesar's Camp, Wimbledon, Surrey, the excavation of 1937' *Archaeol J* 102, 15-20.

Lyne, M, and Jeffries, R, 1979 *The Alice Holt/Farnham Roman Pottery Industry* CBA Research Report 30.

Merriman, N, 1990 *Prehistoric London*.

Museum of London Archaeology Service 2000 *The Archaeology of Greater London: An assessment of archaeological evidence for human presence in the area now covered by Greater London*.

Needham, S, 1987 'The Bronze Age' in Bird, J and Bird, D (eds) 1987, 97-138.

Needham, S, 2008 '800 BC The Great Divide' in Haselgrove and Pope (eds) 2008, 39-63.

Needham, S, and Burgess, C, 1980 'The later Bronze Age in the lower Thames Valley: the metalwork evidence' in Barrett, J and Bradley, R (eds) 1980, 437-70.

O'Connor, B, 1980 *Cross-Channel Relations in the Later Bronze Age* British Archaeol Report International Series 91.

Perry, J, and Skelton, A, 1996 *Evaluation Report on the Prospect Reach Foreshore* (PPT 95) Sutton Archaeological Services, unpublished report.

Pollard, J (ed), 2008 *Prehistoric Britain*.

Quilliec, B, 2008 'Patterns of use and damage in Atlantic swords' in Harmon and Quilliec (eds) 2008, 67-78.

Rackham, J, and Scaife, R, 1997 *Point Pleasant, Wandsworth, PPT95* The Environmental Archaeology Consultancy, unpublished report.

Rackham, J, and Sidell, J, 2000 'London's Landscapes: the changing environment' in Museum of London Archaeology Service 2000, 12-27.

Rowlands, M, 1976 *The Organization of Middle Bronze Age Metalworking* British Archaeol Report 31.

Schulting, R, 2008 'Foodways and Social Ecologies from the Early Mesolithic to the Early Bronze Age' in Pollard (ed) 2008, 90-120.

Sidell, J, 2007 'London: the backwater of Neolithic Britain?' in Sidell and Haughey (eds) 2007, 71-85.

Sidell, J, 2008 'Londinium's Landscape' in Clark *et al* (eds) 2008, 62-68.

Sidell, J, and Haughey, F (eds), 2007 *Neolithic Archaeology in the Intertidal Zone* Neolithic Studies Group Seminar Papers 8.

Sidell, J, and Wilkinson, K, 2004 'The central London Thames: Neolithic river development and flood plain archaeology' in Cotton and Field (eds) 2004, 38-49.

Sidell, J, Wilkinson, K, Scaife, R, and Cameron, N (eds), 2000 *The Holocene Evolution of the Thames* Museum of London Archaeology Service Monograph 5.

Slade, J, 1979 'Spring Passage, Putney' *Wandsworth Historian* 22, 1-2.

Slade, J, 1980 'Venus After Bathing' *Wandsworth Historian* 28, 3.

Sumbler, M (ed), 1996 *British Regional Geology: London and the Thames Valley* British Geological Survey 4th edn.

Sumbler, M, Bridgland, D, Wymer, J, and Balson, P, 1996 'Quaternary' chapter 9 in Sumbler (ed) 1996, 110-136.

Tyers, P, 'Potsherd: *Atlas of Roman Pottery: Britannia'* updated version of his Atlas of Roman Pottery 1996, at website: http:/www.potsherd.uklinux.net/atlas/Source/BRIT.php

Warren, S, 1971 'Neolithic Putney' *London Archaeologist* 1.12, 276-279.

Warren, S, 1977 Excavation of a Neolithic site at Sefton Street, Putney, London *Trans London Middlesex Archaeol Soc* 28, 1-13.

Webley, L, Timby, J and Wilson, M, 2007 *Fairfield Park: Later Prehistoric Settlement in the Eastern Chilterns* Bedfordshire Archaeol Monograph 7.

Wilkinson, K, Scaife, R, Sidell, J, and Cameron, N, 2000 'The palaeoenvironmental context of the JLE project' in Sidell *et al* (eds) 2000, 11-19.

Wymer, J, 1968 *Lower Palaeolithic Archaeology in Britain: as represented by the Thames Valley.*

Wymer, J, 1977 *Gazetteer of Mesolithic Sites in England and Wales* CBA Research Report 20.

Wymer, J, 1991 'The Lower Palaeolithic of the London region' *Trans London Middlesex Archaeol Soc* 42, 1-15.

Wymer, J, 1999 *The Lower Palaeolithic Occupation of Britain.*

2. The Middle Ages

[1] The Venerable Bede *The Ecclesiastical History of the English Nation* Everyman Edition 1958 p165

[2] *The Place Names of Surrey* English Place Name Society 1934

[3] *Wandsworth Historical Society, News sheet 1970 No. 90*

3. Putney Under the Tudors

[1] *Foreign and Domestic Letters and Papers of the Reign of Henry VIII* London 1864 Vol V p.755

[2] *Foreign and Domestic Letters* Vol XIX Part 2, p.405, op cit

[3] A Chasemore *The History and Associations of the Old Bridge at Fulham and Putney* London 1875 p.2

[4] Wandsworth Historical Society, News sheet 1967 No.5

[5] E W Brayley *A History of Surrey* c1880 Vol 3

[6] Sir Walter Besant *London South of the Thames* London 1912 p.2

[7] *Foreign and Domestic Letters* Vol XIV Part 2, op cit

[8] G Cavendish *Life and Death of Cardinal Wolsey* c1555 quoted in Wandsworth Historical Society, News sheet 1969 No.

[9] *Victoria History of the Counties of England History of Surrey* London 1912 Vol IV p81

[10] *Foreign and Domestic Letters* Vol XXI Part 2 item 769, op cit

[11] G E Mitton and J C Geikie *The Fascination of London – Hammersmith, Fulham and Putney* London 1903

4. Parish and Parks

[1] Bill of Complaint, Peek versus Earl Spencer filed in chancery 1 December 1866

[2] Metropolitan Borough of Wandsworth *Official Guide* 1939

[3] Chasemore op cit

[4] Edward Hyde *History of the Rebellion quoted in A History of Richmond Park* by C L Collenette London 1937 pp.5-6

[5] Hyde op cit

5.The Putney Debates 1647
[1] Colonel Rainsborough, The Putney Debates 1647 – inscribed over the entrance to St Mary's church

Sources
Dorian Gerhold *The Putney Debates 1647* 2007
The Clarke Papers I, II edit. C H Firth Camden Society 2nd Series 1891
Tristram Hunt *English Civil War at first-hand* Weidenfeld and Nicholson 2002
Michael Mendle *Putney Debates of 1647: the army, the Levellers* Cambridge University Press 2001
John Morrill FBA *Reactions to the English Civil War 1642-1649* Macmillan 1982
Geoffrey Robertson *The Putney Debates* Verso 2007
Austin Woolrych FBA *Soldiers and statesmen: the General Council of the Army and its debates, 1647-1647* Oxford 1987

6. To Build a Bridge?
[1] Anchitell Grey *Debates of the House of Commons from the Year 1667 to the Year 1694* London 1769 pp415-417

[2] Chasemore op cit p31

[3] C G Harper *The Portsmouth Road* London 1895 pp10-11

[4] Green op cit

[5] *Notes and Queries* 30 March 1895 pp248-249

[6] *Notes and Queries* 30 March 1895 pp248-249

[7] Besant op cit p214

[8] Chasemore op cit

[9] Harper op cit p12

[10] Hugh Phillips *The Thames about 1750* London 1951 pp170-171

[11] Lysons op cit p426

7. Highways, Travellers and Highwaymen
[1] The National Archives SP 25/27 Part 1

[2] Richard Phillips *A Morning's Walk from London to Kew* London 1820 pp125-6

[3] C J Fèret Fulham Old and New 1900 vol 1 p61

[4] London Metropolitan Archives P95/MRY1/414 ff177-185

[5] C T Davis *Notabilities* Putney Newsletter 1912

[6] *Local Enquiries* Wandsworth Heritage Service

8. Roehampton 15th to 21st Century
[1] Richard Phillips op cit

[2] Besant op cit p.220

[3] Richard Phillips op cit pp141-44

[4] I Ivimey *Who slept Here?* London 1961 p.73

9. Growth Begins
[1] E W Brayley *A History of Surrey* c1880

[2] Sir Niklaus Pevsner *London* London 1952 Vol 2

[3] *Victoria County Histories* op cit pp82-83

[4] J S Winter *Beautiful Jim* quoted in the Wandsworth Borough News 16 August 1909

[5] Edward Carter *The Future of London* London 1962 p14

[6] G A Sekon *The London and South Western Railway – Half a Century of Railway Progress* London 1896 p17

[7] H P White *A Regional History of the Railways of Great Britain* London 1963 Vol III pp40-41

[8] National Census Returns 1801 and 1871

[9] *Victoria County Histories* op cit p83

[10] R L Green ed London 1953

[11] Mitton and Geikie op cit

[12] B E Cracknell *Portrait of London River* London 1968 p74

[13] Mitton and Geikie op cit p82

[14] Letter in *The Putney Newsletter* 13 January 1912

Source
Jacqueline Loose *Roehampton the last village in London* London Borough of Wandsworth Libraries and Arts 1979

10. Saving the Commons
[1] Charles Dickens ed *All the Year Round* 17 August 1867 pp191-2

[2] R Sisley *The London Water Supply: A Retrospect and a Survey* London 1899

11. Literature and Leisure
[1] Winifred Whitehead *Wimbledon 1885-1965* [undated] p6

[2] A H Hyamson *Dictionary of English Phrases* London 1922

[3] Rev Blomfield Jackson *Putney, Past and Present* London 1883 pp38-9

[4] *Notes and Queries* 19 August 1882 p149

[5] Passengers could generally identify the route of a bus by the colour of the vehicle. According to Baedeker's *London and its Environs* (1900 ed.), p. 36, the City terminus of this service was Liverpool Street.

[6] A point of some historical interest. For those who do not know it, the railway bridge is, and for many years has been, a deep pea-green colour.

[7] Neil Robson Wandsworth Historical Society Newsletter, Autumn 2004

[8] Sir Osbert Lancaster *All Done from Memory* London 1963

Sources
Pat Heery *Putney Velodrome and the Velodrome Estate* K & N Press 1999
Patrick Loobey *Cinemas and Theatres of Wandsworth and Battersea* Tempus 2004

12. Putney at War 1939-45
[1] Wandsworth Historian

Sources
Anthony Shaw and Jon Mills *We Served-War Time Wandsworth and Battersea* Wandsworth Borough Council
Geoffery Haines *Notes and Diaries* Wandsworth Heritage Centre, Johns Hill
Vivienne Hall *Diaries* Imperial war Museum
Personal interviews with Sheila Monagahan, Tony Pink, Christine Sand Wandsworth Historian Wandsworth Historical Society
Patrick Loobey and Jon Mills *The Boroughs of Wandsworth and Battersea at War* Sutton Publishing